HONKY-TONK
GOSPEL

HONKY-TONK GOSPEL

THE STORY OF SIN
AND SALVATION
IN COUNTRY MUSIC

**Gene Edward Veith
and
Thomas L. Wilmeth**

Baker Books
A Division of Baker Book House Co
Grand Rapids, Michigan 49516

Published by Baker Books
a division of Baker Book House Company
P.O. Box 6287, Grand Rapids, MI 49516-6287

Printed in the United States of America

Library of Congress Cataloging-in-Publication Data

Veith, Gene Edward, 1951–
    Honky-tonk gospel : the story of sin and salvation in country music / Gene Edward Veith and Thomas L. Wilmeth.
        p.   cm.
    ISBN 0-8010-6355-8 (paper)
    1. Country music—Religious aspects—Christianity. 2. Country music—Social aspects. 3. Country music—History and criticism. I. Wilmeth, Thomas L. II. Title.
ML3524.V45   2001
261.5'78—dc21   00-065178

Scripture is from the King James Version of the Bible.

For current information about all releases from Baker Book House, visit our web site: http://www.bakerbooks.com

Contents

1. The Music of American Adults   9
2. Gospel Music Origins: Blood Songs
   and Testimonies   17
3. The Bristol Sessions: The Carter Family and Jimmie
   Rodgers   25
4. Nashville: From the Opry to the Outlaws   47
5. The Christian Tradition in Country Music: Between
   the Devil and Me   71
6. The Christian Tradition in Country Music: Old Ruined
   Churches   89
7. Country Music's Moral Tradition: Marriage
   and D-I-V-O-R-C-E   103
8. Country Music's Moral Tradition: Drinkin', Cheatin',
   and Family Values   121
9. The Country Artist: Hank Williams versus Luke
   the Drifter   135
10. Contemporary Country Music   155

   Notes   183
   Credits and Acknowledgments   187

This book is dedicated to Charles and Violet Sutton, who used to hear Bob Wills at the Cain Ballroom, and who exposed their grandson to this kind of music at an age when he was predisposed to hate it. Also to Imogene Wilmeth and Ramona Ruch.

1

The Music
of American Adults

All distinctly American music originates
from poor people in the South. America's
most seminal musical art form was the
blues, the invention of black slaves and
sharecroppers. When these same African
Americans migrated to the big cities, their
musical tradition mutated into jazz, in all
its forms. Poor white people of the hills, the
coal mines, and the sharecropper fields
were also making music. The roots of this
music can be traced to the folk ballads of
the British Isles, but it soon acquired its own
Appalachian tones and variations and further developed into the various strains of
country music.

Rock and roll gets the most attention today, as the exemplar of American popular music. Country music gets little notice from cultural critics. When *Entertainment Weekly* listed its Top 100 musical events of the century, country music was nowhere to be found. For this poll and many like it, rock and roll was the only genre that counted. But rock and roll itself can be described as the fusion of the music of poor blacks with that of poor whites.

This cultural synthesis was achieved largely by one person—Elvis Presley. Elvis Presley was listed prominently on all the millennium lists, ranking third on the *Entertainment Weekly* list, behind only the Beatles and Chuck Berry. Elvis placed second in *Entertainment Weekly*'s list of the century's top entertainers (a category that had no room for country stars such as Hank Williams and Patsy Cline). Elvis was ranked first in *People Magazine*'s list of favorite male pop stars. Elvis Presley, though, was a truck driver from Memphis who performed on the Grand Ole Opry and is a member of the Country Music Hall of Fame. What he—and other "rockabilly" acts—pulled off was to bring into country and western music the African-American form of rhythm and blues.

When the blues went into the big cities, it took on a dance beat and a horn section, eventually attracting white teenagers as well as blacks. While rhythm and blues—as well as jazz and swing music—was driven mostly by wind instruments, the country tradition favored strings, especially the guitar. Black rural bluesmen also played the guitar, but when the music went to the city, it took on the trumpet and the saxophone. Elvis sang rhythm and blues that was guitar-driven. His rock and roll also had country flavorings—including backup singers that were members of a gospel quartet, the Jordanaires. That the guitar became the signature instrument of rock and roll is only one mark of country music's influence, even on its rock competitors.

Elvis was criticized by Jim Crow Southern racists for mingling black music with white music. But ironically, country music itself came into being through a similar synthesis. Back in the 1920s, Jimmie Rodgers, who was hailed as the father of country music, combined black rural blues with the balladry of the white working class. This is evident in his trademark "blue yodels," which consist of a western-style yodel added to hard-core twelve-bar blues. Rodgers as well was criticized in his time for his use of black music—he went so far as to add Dixieland horns to his strummed guitar and actually recorded with Louis Armstrong.

America's music has roots set deep into the culture of people—white and black—who knew suffering and poverty, who had to work hard with little to show for it, who were outside the mainstream of the social elite, who were largely uneducated, but who found expression for their lives in music. Odd as it may seem, but befitting a democracy, music that originated from the socially marginal would become, with the advent of the mass media—the technology to record and sell and broadcast individual performances—the most popular musical forms for the whole nation, if not the whole world.

Though largely overlooked by the cultural elite, country music continues to have a life of its own. Its appeal now seems to transcend social and economic class. Data from the Simmons Study of Media and Markets show that in 1997, 40 percent of individuals earning over $40,000 per year and 33 percent of those who earn over $100,000 listen to country. In fact, statistics show country fans to be more educated than either adult contemporary or rock audiences. Thirty-six percent of country fans have a college degree, as opposed to 30 percent for adult contemporary and 22 percent for rock fans.[1]

Country music is the top radio format in America, with nearly 2,500 stations. (Adult contemporary comes in second with 1,500 stations.) Forty-two percent of all radio listeners tune in to country music, which is also the top-rated format in fifty-five of the nation's one hundred largest cities, including Washington, D.C., and Seattle.

Country music is still second to rock and roll in total album sales, in 1997 making up 14 percent of the market compared to rock's 26 percent. Though rock fans buy more albums than country fans, sales for country music have almost doubled over the last decade, while rock is down over 40 percent since 1989. Country's 14 percent market share tops rhythm and blues (13 percent) and rap (10 percent). Despite a dearth of black performers (except for some notable exceptions such as Charlie Pride), as many as 25 percent of African Americans over eighteen listen to country.

Teenagers have been defecting from rock to country in large numbers. Since 1988, the percentage of teenagers preferring country music has tripled. Forty-three percent of young Americans between eighteen and twenty-four now listen to country. But perhaps the most significant demographic is that country is the most popular music among women over thirty.

Country is music for adults. Rock and roll is about adolescents—their young loves and lusts, their rebellions, and their insecurities. No such generation gap exists in country music. The same stars appeal to all age groups, and a typical country music concert is attended by grandparents, parents, teenagers, and children. But in spite of this intergenerational appeal, country music sings about adult concerns: marriage, work, children, memories. It also sings frankly and poignantly about adult problems: divorce, single parenthood, alcoholism, job woes, money worries, loneliness, death.

"You've probably got to be twenty-four or twenty-five to even understand a country song," observes Lon Helton, country editor of *Radio & Records*. "Life has to slap you around a little bit, and then you go, 'Now I get what they're singing about.'"

The hallmark of country music is authenticity. Country music, in the words of George Jones, is "real people singing real songs about real life for real people." From its down-to-earth musical traditionalism to its agonizingly honest lyrics, country music evokes a sense of realism. Though its words may be humorous and self-mocking or sentimental and preachy, country music, perhaps more often than not, is about suffering. Part of its aesthetic appeal is as a catalyst for empathy. "Country music in its purest form forges an iron-grip bond with the listener, a connection that stems from sharing everyday experiences," says Dallas music critic Mario Tarradell. "In essence, it's real life with a steel guitar crying in the background."

The real world for country music includes Christianity. In stark contrast to most of today's other entertainment venues, people in country songs are likely to pray, quote the Bible, and talk about Jesus. This is true not only in country's most traditional forms, such as bluegrass, in which every other song in a set list may have a Christian theme, and classic country, in which artists always included at least one gospel number in their sets. It is true also in contemporary country music, which in many other ways has drifted far from its roots. In Trisha Yearwood's "Everybody Knows" (Gary Harrison, Matraca Berg)[2] the jilted lover turns to her pastor for advice, just as naturally as she does "the gals at work." In Tracy Byrd's song, a love-struck husband tips his hat to "The Keeper of the Stars" (D. Lee, K. Staley, D. Mayo) for giving him his wife. Vince Gill wrote a poignant and achingly beautiful song on the death of his handicapped brother in "Go Rest High upon That Mountain," about the promise of eternal life "with the Father and the Son." Country music has a way of bringing God into the picture in a serious but natural way.

Not that country music is always pious. In fact, teenage rock fans, when their country-loving parents get on their case, can often turn the tables by drawing attention to what their parents are listening to. Rock music may have sexual innuendos, but country music, in its down-to-earth way, is often even more explicit about sex. Garth Brooks sings about marital fidelity and thanks God for unanswered prayers, but he also sings about a boy's first sexual experience and one-night stands. Reba McIntire's "Fancy" (Bobbie Gentry) is a chilling song about a woman selling her daughter into prostitution—though far from being an example of contemporary permissiveness in popular music, Reba's version is a remake of a tune Lynn Anderson recorded decades ago. Reba's "Little Rock" (Pat McManus, Quentin Powers) is a breathtaking trivialization of adultery, as a woman—to a lighthearted melody—takes off her wedding ring for a night of unfaithfulness.

Rock may have veiled references to drugs, but that may pale compared to the substance abuse—namely, alcohol—sung about in country music. Heavy metal and rap may sing about violence, but they are seldom as bloodcurdling as an Appalachian murder ballad.

For all of its apparent conservatism, country music reflects the changes and conflicts in American culture. The breakdown of the American family—and its emotional consequences—can be traced in the lyrics of country music, from Tammy Wynette's "D-I-V-O-R-C-E" (Braddock, Putman Jr.) to the current laments about divorced fathers missing their children. It is one thing for the cultural elite to champion feminism, but when Martina McBride sings about "Independence Day" (Gretchen Peters) and Reba McIntire asks "Is There Life Out There?" (Susan Longacre, Rick Giles) beyond family and home, it is evident that feminism has taken deep root in the assumptions of ordinary Americans. The same is true for homosexuality. Garth Brooks recorded a song defending the right of people to love whomever they want, and at country music awards shows stars now routinely wear AIDS ribbons.

Even the more esoteric of contemporary ideas are showing up in country music. A hit by the group Diamond Rio sings "It's All in Your Head" (Tony Martin, Van Stephenson, Reese Wilson) about a preacher's conspiracy theories. The chorus asserts the unknowability of truth: "It's all interpretation!" When postmodernism can be found even in country music, it is a sign of how deeply it has permeated the American mind.

And yet, Diamond Rio's invocation of relativism is countered by Patty Loveless singing "The Trouble with the Truth" (Gary Nicholson), in which she realizes that "the trouble with the truth/Is it's just what I need to hear."

Country music, though sometimes vulgar and rowdy, remains a forum for traditional values. Love songs tend to be directed to one's spouse. While rock and roll may articulate rebellion against parents, parenthood is sacrosanct in country music.

The pathos in country music is most strongly felt when home and family are lost or broken. When country songs deal with divorce, for example, they are characteristically emotionally and morally honest. Though divorce songs from a woman's point of view are sometimes celebrations of independence in a feminist vein, most are wistful meditations in which a woman tells herself—not always convincingly—that "I can get through this." Similar songs from a man's point of view are almost always full of anguished regret—the man drives his pickup through the old neighborhood, sees his wife with another man, and realizes that he will never see his children grow up. There are also songs that beg for forgiveness, such as Trisha Yearwood's "Believe Me Baby, I Lied" (Kim Richie, Larry Gottlieb, Angelo Petraglia) and Wade Hayes' "What I Meant to Say" (Cook, Hogin, McBride). In the world of country music, actions have consequences, which are portrayed with emotional and moral realism.

The worldview of country music embraces both sin and grace. Historically, country music grew out of both little country churches and honky-tonks, family sing-alongs and drunken Saturday nights. Expressions of both sides of life—and the conflict between them—can still be found in country music. Many of its greatest artists were consumed by the internal battle between sin and grace, as was the case with Hank Williams, who poured himself out in songs of bleak despair ("Alone and Forsaken") and in songs that cling desperately to Christ ("I Saw the Light").

This book will explore the Christian dimension of country music. This does not mean that we will simply extract edifying verses from country music lyrics. Christianity is not a matter of moralism or positive messages. Rather, it is about the salvation of people who need salvation. Country music, unlike other popular art forms, has a way of acknowledging the sinfulness of sin. And though it sometimes goes too far in wallowing in that sin, at some point—unlike other popular art forms—it has a way of acknowledging the power of the gospel.

Christianity constitutes a worldview, a perspective that embraces all of life. Therefore, a Christian examination of a particular musical genre will attend to worldview issues, both those that correspond to and those that depart from the biblical sense of life. Country music, emerging as it has from the deepest roots of American folk culture, is perhaps a surer guide to the inner workings of American values than other art forms that have attracted more attention. Another theme of this book is how country music has reflected our cultural problems, from

the breakdown of the family to the bland, content-free con-
sumerism of the popular culture. Nevertheless, country music—
in its range, its authenticity, and its numerous artists who have
been believing Christians—suggests something of what a biblical worldview might mean for the arts.

Johnny Cash—the legendary "Man in Black" who, after his
conversion to Christ, wrote his testimony in *The Man in White*—
lists in the liner notes to his album *Unchained* what he likes in
music:

> I love songs about horses, railroads, land, judgment day, family,
> hard times, whiskey, courtship, marriage, adultery, separation,
> murder, war, prison, rambling, damnation, home, salvation,
> death, pride, humor, piety, rebellion, patriotism, larceny, deter-
> mination, tragedy, rowdiness, heartbreak, and love. And Mother.
> And God.[3]

Spiritual concerns jostle with earthly concerns. They are not
separated or compartmentalized. Land and judgment day, rambling and damnation, murder and piety, rowdiness and salvation—the spirituality here is not some gnostic otherworldly
mysticism but something grounded in the tangible facts of ordinary life. And ordinary life—which includes transgressions and
suffering as well as pleasures and comforting relationships—
has eternal significance. Except for the railroads, Cash could
be describing much of what is in the Bible.

2

Gospel Music Origins

BLOOD SONGS AND TESTIMONIES

Nearly every country music artist—at least those whose careers span a number of albums—at some point records a gospel album.[1] "While country music has changed radically during its sixty-year commercial history," comments country music scholar Bill Malone, "the singing of gospel songs has remained a constant in the lives of its performers. Such superstars as Merle Haggard, Willie Nelson, and Loretta Lynn routinely record entire albums devoted to the genre, and even the most sophisticated of writers, Kris Kristofferson, writes and records religious songs that become commercial hits" (for example, "Why Me, Lord" and "One Day at a Time").[2]

Similarly, in country music performances, sets typically include a sacred number, often as the final word. This custom has been honored at concerts, TV shows, the early radio broadcasts and, according to Dorothy Horstman, goes back to the very earliest traditions of country music.[3] She goes on to comment that nearly all of the country music singers she interviewed for her book said that gospel music—singing in church, learning the old hymns, growing up with Christian music—had been an important part of their lives.[4] And, in many cases, it still is.

The persistence of explicitly Christian numbers in the repertoire of most country singers—even those with hell-raising reputations—is probably because many were raised in Southern evangelical churches. The same could be said of the whole musical tradition of country music; its history, its artists, and its audience have all been shaped by evangelical Protestantism. Moreover, this influence is not easily set aside, despite the wild living represented by the beer joints and honky-tonks that have been country music's bread and butter.

Ultimately, Christianity keeps showing up in country music because of the faith of its performers. Don Cusic refers to

> the deep-seated faith that rests in the hearts of many country music artists. Ironically, it is a faith at odds with that of most contemporary music. Country artists do songs about cheating, drinking, hurting, and loving because they are a reflection of life. Many do gospel music for the same reason. For them, the Gospel is part of life too.[5]

Bill Malone goes even further, seeing Christianity in the attitudes, the themes, and the total worldview of even the most seemingly secular country music:

> Religion has been a profound influence in shaping the content, styles, and general mood of country music. Rural and working-class Southerners, who comprised the bulk of country music's original audience and who indeed created the music in the first place, grew up in a region dominated by fundamentalist Protes-

tantism. The belief in a personal God, the certainty of rewards and punishments, and the rejection of a lost and dying world became part of a total world view which affected even the secular music they made. The sense of fatalism, guilt and consciousness of sin that colors the lyrics of love songs, and even beer-drinking songs, is in large part religion-derived.[6]

Charlie Louvin—who with his brother Ira (the Louvin Brothers), paired precursors of rock and roll with searing fundamentalist gospel their whole career—tells how, when the bars he played in would close, the drunks would typically gather around to sing some hymns, a sobering-up time of repentance after the night's debauch.[7] Cusic observes that

> Gospel is the conscience of country music, and woven into the hell-raisin' shenanigans many country artists sing about is the thread of belief in God and the forgiveness of sins. They seem to admit their sins and hope for a righteous life while at the same time confessing they can't obtain it. So the vicious cycle of sin and salvation spins round and round.[8]

But it isn't a vicious cycle; it is the primal conflict between sin and grace, the battle played out in the human soul, described in the Bible—and fundamentalist churches—as the human condition.

From Gospel to Country

As far back as 1770, churches in the South were sponsoring singing schools, in which members would gather to learn how to sing. The shape-note tradition taught even unlettered people how to read music—using a musical transcription that portrayed the fa-so-la tones with different shapes, in addition to their usual placement on the staff—resulting in what music historians calls a major democratization of music.[9]

The so-called Sacred Harp tradition, named for the title of a popular songbook, was a means of devotion, meditation, and fellowship with other Christians. This music was not originally sung for Sunday worship, choir practice, or special music for church. "Sacred Harp has never been a 'performance' kind of music. The singers are not arranged in a line or a semi-circle facing the audience. Instead the circle or square is closed, and the singers face each other."[10] The goal was never to stand out as a solo performer or to excel to impress people, whether at church or elsewhere. The singers faced each other so they could hear their voices blend. They were singing to God and to each other. Harmony was both the musical goal and the spiritual goal.

In these singing groups, church members would get together to sing, just as they might get together for Bible study or prayer group. Though these songs influenced what would later be sung in the sanctuary, from the beginning they had a life of their own outside of the church.

When people got together to play musical instruments, they also stood in a circle so they could hear each other and blend in—an act of communal, participatory music-making, not a performance before a passive, non-music-making audience. This is still the practice today when people come together to play bluegrass music.

It was in these circles, both those of Christian song and those of fiddle and guitar, that the sounds of country music were born. The tones, the melodies, and especially the harmonies were perfected. Certainly, the old folk ballads were part of the mix— the variations on tunes and stories that go back for centuries to European forebears—but it was the pursuit of sacred music, self-consciously learned and practiced, that developed into an art form.

The nineteenth century saw the rise of camp meetings, evangelistic revivals that began to feature songs from this tradition of popular Christian piety. Out of these revivals came the term "gospel music." This referred specifically to songs that carried an evangelistic message—the salvation of sinners through Christ. Gospel songs typically followed the pattern of the other evangelistic messages that were proclaimed at these meetings: the personal testimony, a narrative of confession in which a Christian told about his life of sin and his conversion through faith in Christ.

The evangelistic camp meetings were not the same as church services. The former were directed at nonbelievers (though Christians from many different church bodies attended them in droves). These were not construed as worship services but as outreach tools. The emotional, informal, and highly personal evangelism services, held outside the church in tents, were distinct from the more formal and traditional liturgies of the worship services in church.

Denominations with strong theologies of worship—such as Presbyterian and Episcopalian—kept the distinction of their formal liturgies. But with the rise of the Pentecostal movement in the early twentieth century and the emphasis on revivals among Baptists, Methodists, and other groups, the line between the camp meeting and the church service began to blur. In the controversies over what music was appropriate for what purpose, the musical genres became further refined. Hymns were understood as being directed upward, from the human being to God. Gospel music, on the other hand, was directed outward, from one human being to another. One early preacher, the Reverend Phil Kerr, put it this way: "A hymn is a *prayer* set to music," and should be sung reverently. "A gospel song is a *testimony* or *exhortation,* set to music" and should be sung "with the same enthusiasm and earnestness and victory with which a testimony or exhortation would be delivered."[11]

Country music might be defined as secularized testimony. As country artists continually point out, country songs tend to be stories. A group of songwriters recently commented that when the desire is to tell a story, the song usually comes out as a country song. Pop music for the radio depends on catchy musical hooks; dance music is all rhythm and hooks; narratives, though, go with country.[12] Country songs tend to be well-spun tales and dramatic monologues, little fictions complete with a plot, characters, and denouement. Though fictionalized, they usually present a persona who tells a story of his or her life, often a painful tale of loss, loneliness, and regret—or as in the old gospel songs, a life of sin.

Sometimes these narratives affirm some hard-won lesson in life, addressing the listener with some bit of wisdom or advice.

That is to say, they are personal exhortations. And the Reverend Phil Kerr's criteria for enthusiasm and earnestness—though victory is far less seldom—still apply.

Blood Songs

Early gospel music was not just vapid piety. Gospel songs tended to be forceful, dramatic stories about temptation, backsliding, death, damnation, and being washed clean in the blood of Jesus. They were down-to-earth, real-to-life narratives that never flinched from the dark side of the human condition, songs often described as "blood songs."

The Louvin Brothers, as late as 1959, recorded an album that included many such blood songs, entitled *Satan Is Real*. It includes such harrowing songs as "Dying from Home, and Lost," "The Drunkard's Doom," and "Satan's Jeweled Crown." Not that everything is brimstone. The album also includes songs of grace and salvation, such as "The Angels Rejoiced Last Night," "The River of Jordan," and "He Can Be Found." There is also the pointed evangelism of "Are You Afraid to Die?" Perhaps the most representative of the genre is the old tune popularized by the Carter Family, "The Kneeling Drunkard's Plea," about a drunk at the end of his rope turning in repentance to Christ.

Gospel music soon developed an appeal outside the context of church. With the advent of recording technology and the radio, it even acquired commercial value. Bill Malone chronicles how gospel quartets achieved commercial success, followed by brother duets. From the Delmore Brothers through the Louvin Brothers—who kept their gospel roots even while breaking new ground in popular music—to the Everly Brothers and the transition to rock and roll, the brother groups played an important role in American music.

The Chuck Wagon Gang, however, was the most important bridge, according to Malone, between gospel and country music. They sang songs of faith, and they sang songs about ordinary life, with no sense of contradiction. Other early performers did the same. Often one side of a record was a love song, and the other side was a gospel song.

But before long, gospel and country—while remaining related—started going their separate ways. As country music became more and more commercially successful, one could argue that it became more worldly. Some audiences, on both sides, became squeamish about mixing the sacred and the secular. With Prohibition and the rise of a more anticultural fundamentalism, the two major institutions of rural communities—the church and the tavern—grew farther apart. And the latter had the jukeboxes and invited country music bands to play for their dances. The revelers didn't necessarily want to hear about Jesus while they were having a good time. "As country music emerged as a music for honky tonks and beer joints," says Don Cusic, "there was a reluctance by these patrons to hear a gospel song on the jukebox because of the conviction and guilt it would bring."[13] Thus the perennial issue for Southern preachers about where their members were Saturday night as opposed to where they were Sunday morning; but there was a reason why they were in church, despite their hangovers. Sin needed to be followed by repentance.

Eventually, two different markets emerged, with the stricter churchgoers restricting their tastes to gospel music—despite the fact that gospel music was originally written specifically for unbelievers, with a view to evangelize them. While country music kept its ties to the old-time religious music, and gospel in turn became more commercial—and as American Christianity lost its theological intensity—gospel music began to lose its edge. Groups such as the Happy Goodman Family began to stress happy, optimistic, inspirational, and uplifting songs about moralism and sentimental family values, as opposed to the blood songs of tragedy, repentance, and bloody redemption.

According to Bill Malone, there are more genuinely fundamentalist themes, more of the earnest, honest, emotionally searing blood songs in country music than in today's sanitized gospel music.

Country singers are much more likely to sing the old-time "blood songs" and world-rejection songs of early Protestantism than are the gospel singers. As gospel music has prospered and fused more directly with pop music, it has shorn itself of the sectarianism that once gave it strength and identity. If one would hear the dogmas of old-fashioned fundamentalism, with both their strengths and their weaknesses, he need look no farther than the recordings of the Louvin Brothers or the Bailes Brothers, or to the compositions of someone like Mac Odell.[14]

Malone also notes that "today, even mainstream country musicians have diluted the theology and softened the passion of the gospel songs they sing. Bluegrass music, though, has remained a repository of the older songs and styles."[15] Nevertheless, for blood songs—dogmatic or not, or fully resolved by the gospel or not—one might turn to the testimonies of Hank Williams, Merle Haggard, Johnny Cash, George Jones, Reba McIntire, or just about anyone else in their train.

3

The Bristol Sessions

THE CARTER FAMILY AND JIMMIE RODGERS

Country music advanced from individual backwoods performances to a mass-produced national art form in the summer of 1927, when a New York producer in the then-infant recording industry came to the small town of Bristol on the Tennessee-Kentucky border to audition local acts for a national audience. These so-called Bristol Sessions, according to Johnny Cash, "are the single most important event in the history of country music."[1] Nearly every element of what country music would become was to be found in these auditions (which have been preserved in a recording, *The Bristol Sessions*, by the Country Music Foundation and can still be listened to today). Among other things, the Bristol Sessions marked the discovery of the two defining talents of country music, performers who embodied both extremes of country music themes, from pious songs of hearth and home to the self-destructive license of the honky-tonk attitude. The Bristol Sessions launched the careers of the Carter Family and Jimmie Rodgers.

Just as the town of Bristol is partly in Tennessee and partly in Kentucky, the Bristol Sessions themselves would come to be a dividing line and crossroads in its own right. Jimmie Rodgers' biographer Nolan Porterfield states that the Bristol Sessions of 1927 "have come to signal the Big Bang of country music evolution," but is equally quick to note that "the idea [of Bristol as] the place where it all started . . . is oversimplified, but it works."[2]

The Bristol Sessions were arranged by distant New York City's Victor Records (now RCA Victor), which was just one of several companies sending men with recording equipment out into the field to find and record hillbilly music. The companies wanted to take advantage of the sales generated by the very first country records made by hillbilly performers who had recently shown that this sort of music had surprisingly large sales potential.

Ralph Peer had shown special talent for these recording trips. In 1923 Peer had gone to the South on such a field trip for Okeh Records. In Atlanta, Georgia, he recorded Fiddlin' John Carson performing "The Little Log Cabin in the Lane." This record, in effect, gave birth to commercial country music by becoming a huge seller, a fact that dumbfounded the businessmen of the recording world.[3] This unexpected blip on the sales ledgers made the record companies take notice. Then in 1924, when singer Vernon Dalhart sold over one million copies of the plaintive tale "The Prisoner's Song" for Victor, the company's economic appetite was whetted, and exploratory expeditions were planned to find performers capable of duplicating this type of bottom-line profit.

Victor Records wanted Peer to repeat the success he had achieved with Carson's record for Okeh, capitalizing on Dalhart's largely untapped audience. He was to scour the South and the mountain region for music that would sell in large quantities. The goal was not to document the music of the backwoods farmer and mountaineer for the sake of preserving history. That task would be taken up decades later by Alan Lomax and others for the Smithsonian Institute. Victor's goals were less altruistic; they sent Peer on the road to find material that would sell and make the company money.

Although not the absolute starting place for commercial country music, there is good reason for the Bristol Sessions to be heralded as a touchstone for the form. It is uniquely important for first discovering two major recording stars, popular during their own day and influential for decades beyond. Peer did not travel to Bristol with the intention of meeting and recording both Jimmie Rodgers and the great Carter Family. But he did. Victor had hoped that Peer would find another Fiddlin' John Carson. Instead, he made the first recordings of two of the most noteworthy acts in country music history. And more to the point for Victor, they sold lots of records, establishing country music not only as an art form but as an industry, a player in the newly emerging American mass culture.

Like the music he recorded, the people Ralph Peer heard in late July and early August of 1927 were a mix. Some were regionally known performers who had been contacted about coming to Bristol. Peer seems to have arranged about half of his recording appointments before arriving in Bristol, leaving the other half to be filled with local talent who could audition for their big break. Even in 1927, it was known that a big-selling record could make a lot of money for the performer. Scores of musicians—used to picking in their family parlors, singing in church, and playing for hoedowns—left their farms to perform before a microphone for the first time.

It is not surprising that half of the songs recorded were overtly religious. For the people in rural Kentucky and Tennessee, there was no sharp dividing line between the sacred and the secular. The way they sang in church was much the way they sang everywhere else. In the rural South of that day, whether people were singing about the love of Jesus or the love of a bride, the music was essentially the same.

Thus, one of the groups that auditioned during the Bristol Sessions, the Tennessee Mountaineers, was actually a church choir. This twenty-member group offered an a cappella rendition of "Standing on the Promises."[4] A staple of Southern church music was the gospel quartet, represented at Bristol by Ernest Phipps and his Holiness Quartet, singing a fervent "I Want to Go Where Jesus Is," and the Alcoa Quartet's formal four-part harmony on "I'm Redeemed."

Then there was Alfred G. Karnes, with his distinct and pleasant vocal style. Like Rodgers, Karnes' diction is precise and one is able to picture the religious scenes he fervently describes. Karnes' topics never strayed from the overtly religious gospel message. This is not surprising since Karnes was a preacher. All of the five songs Karnes recorded with Peer have sacred topics, including "When They Ring the Golden Bells," "To the Work," and "I Am Bound for the Promised Land."

Such explicit gospel songs were mingled on *The Bristol Sessions* with nursery rhymes, lullabies, vivid depictions of train wrecks, comic vignettes of courtship, and murder ballads. The performers included not only church groups and a preacher but also mountaineers, coon hunters, and moonshiners.[5] And they all from time to time sang about Jesus.

One of the best and most melodic of the specifically religious songs is Blind Alfred Reed's "Walking in the Way with Jesus," simultaneously a proclamation of the singer's faith and a lament for lost sinners. Reed is "sick at heart" for all who do not follow His way. Temptation is also present, as the singer openly acknowledges his leanings "to do wrong." But to remedy this, he merely returns to the Lord and asks for protection, whereupon "everything's all right." The confessional attitude is clear as, in the final verse, the singer proclaims that he has given up sin and drinking to walk with Jesus. By God's grace he is saved, joins the angels' choir, and is "feelin' mighty happy now."

The other song that Blind Alfred recorded is about a train wreck. In "The Wreck of the Virginian" he performs solo, with his fiddle for accompaniment. The fiddle lines double the melody being sung, with both voice and fiddle distinct and clear. The moral of this song is that the "ladies whose husband runs an engine on the line" should be prepared for the death of their husbands, so (implicitly) they should treat them well. The note is one that sounds throughout early country music: the fact of mortality. No one knows when the end is approaching, and this could be your last chance to pray, be nice to a person, or ask for forgiveness.

There is another train wreck song on *The Bristol Sessions*, "The Newmarket Wreck"—a rushed, nasal account of a specific train derailment by Mr. and Mrs. J. W. Baker. The motif would be updated later by Roy Acuff's car wreck song, "The Wreck on the Highway" (Dorothy Dixon) with its grisly imagery of "whiskey and blood mixed together" on the pavement—the moral of which is not, as one might expect today, the danger of drinking and driving, but the folly of people who do not take time to pray.

A different kind of train song is offered by The Teneva Ramblers. "The Longest Train I Ever Saw" has remained in country music's collective consciousness, with new versions still being recorded today. Its lyrics describe a railroad en route to heaven. In fact, this imagery appears not only in several numbers recorded at the Bristol Sessions but ever after in Southern gospel and country music, in a whole succession of trains bound for glory. The ideal of freedom and travel to a new place, with the rails taking one to the Holy Land, enabled the transportation technology of the industrial revolution to be construed as a religious symbol.

Picking up the pilgrim motif, Alfred Karnes declares, "I Am Bound for the Promised Land," but doesn't give his method of travel. Perhaps he is planning to board that celestial railroad described by the Teneva Ramblers. In addition to Karnes' strong vocal on "Bound for the Promised Land," an interesting feature of this recording is that Karnes plays the harp-guitar. This odd instrument is about the size of a full-size bass fiddle, with guitar and harp strings attached to different parts of the instrument's body. The performer ostensibly had the ability to both play single line guitar runs and provide his own rhythm backing, which Karnes does. The combination of a guitar with a harp is itself a fitting metaphor for music that tries to be simultaneously earthbound and celestial.[6]

Another family group that got its start at the Bristol Sessions—one that would span successive generations to the point of appearing on television's *The Andy Griffith Show*—was the Stoneman family. The scope of their music is illustrated by the wide range of songs performed, in different ensembles, by the family patriarch Ernest V. Stoneman. The most overtly religious of all the titles recorded at the sessions came from Ernest V. Stoneman and his Dixie Mountaineers. Sounding more like a small church ensemble, the somewhat ragged performance of "The Resurrection" is sincere, although it lacks the force and drive of the best of its genre. Less successful, if equally heartfelt, is the group's rendition of "Are You Washed in the Blood?" The vocals are not particularly compelling, and the group has a halting quality throughout the entire song, as if they are hesitant about what the other members are planning to do next.

Stoneman is not nearly so tentative, however, when he teams with Irma Frost and Eck Dunford in a trio that offers something commonplace in country music—a sense of humor, and a self-effacing one at that. In "The Mountaineer's Courtship," Stoneman and Frost are engaged in a dramatic ballad, consisting of conversation about courtship in alternating verses, as the couple prepares for their wedding. During the instrumental interludes between the call-and-response singing, the third party, Dunford, quietly mutters a series of play-by-play asides about the unlikely situation. Dunford knows what the intended bride will soon discover—that the man wooing her is already married and has six children. A redundant melody line is superceded by the listener's interest in how the scene will play out. All seems fine in the end, with Stoneman and Frost harmonizing well (if a bit stridently) on the closing chorus.

Another intentionally humorous selection, "Old Time Corn Shuckin'," offers a showcase for various acts that had already appeared at the sessions, including the ubiquitous Ernest Stoneman. The tune is a medley in the time-honored genre of the work song—which would continue to be a common preoccupation of country music—ostensibly taking place during a gathering to get the corn shucked, in advance of the evening's dance. But in many ways the pickup group that went by the name of The Blue Ridge Corn Shuckers actually offers an early drinking song—which also would become a major country motif. Between excerpts of "Home Sweet Home," "Rovin' Gambler," "The Ragged Orphan," and "The Ship That Never Returned," which constitute the corn shucking medley, we hear the various participants take swigs off the jug. "Don't drink too much," admonishes the host—a suggestion perhaps either too late or ignored by the others present, judging by the coughing that follows most of the jug sampling. The performance obviously was a conscious effort on Ralph Peer's part to get a hillbilly comedy record made. Other rube comedy numbers—clearly copied here—had sold a lot of records, and despite the condescension and ridicule implicit in the genre, many mountain musicians were willing to play along.

And yet, this song contains a moral core. As the host indicates at the beginning of the song, the gathering occurs so healthy-bodied men of the area can shuck the corn of the "old folks" who are unable to do some of their own work. In this instance, they have gathered to shuck old Uncle Joe Stoot's corn. Certainly this can be seen as a Do Unto Others and Love Thy Neighbor approach to life—even if they are getting smashed in the process.

"Old Time Corn Shuckin'" is also an interesting number for demonstrating the flexibility of the performers and the cross-fertilization that had occurred throughout the recordings. Ernest Stoneman and Eck Dunford are especially flexible in their changing roles of front man to side man.

The flexibility of Ernest Stoneman is evident not only in the corn shucking medley but throughout the sessions. He could sing about his faith in "The Resurrection" and evangelize the lost with "Are You Washed in the Blood?" Then, with no sense of contradiction, he could do humorous songs about drinking and adultery. Like many country music stars to follow, he could also wax sentimental. Perhaps combining the everyday with the religious, "mother songs" were enormously popular. Ernest Stoneman, K. Brewer, and M. Mooney combine the icons of mother and God, in the process discussing the importance of hard work as well. This trio, singing "Tell Mother I Will Meet Her," offers the idealized mother figure—for she is dead and in heaven. Death and mother would be inseparable topics in country music for decades to come.

Many of the numbers recorded at the Bristol Sessions were not so heavy and serious. Children's songs are represented, with Uncle Eck Dunford performing what has since become a childhood standard, "Skip to Ma Lou, My Darling." The Bull Mountain Moonshiners played "Johnny Goodwin," which has the bouncy and repetitive nature of a children's sing-along, much in the manner of "Skip to Ma Lou."

The West Virginia Coon Hunters represented an area largely neglected by modern country music—the instrumental. While a single theme is played again and again (as at a dance), one member of the group offers a bit of spoken commentary. These pieces are all melody and rhythm, for the dominant instrument can't really be called a solo. This became known as the string band sound. (In a string band, when there are vocals, the instruments simply play the same melody as the voice.) Another true instrumental from *The Bristol Sessions* is distinctive for its pure blues structure. El Watson offers a slow "Pot Licker Blues"—another example of the overlap between the music of poor whites and poor blacks.

One other string band selection is from Dad Blackard's Moonshiners, who perform "Sandy River Belle." The vocals are largely mush and make little sense. The melody, however, is quite infectious. This song is a good example of the difference between a string band and the yet-to-be-developed sound of bluegrass. Even though the primary instruments of fiddle and banjo are present and quite audible, there are no solo breaks. Members of a string band usually all played the same melody line—in unison. It would take Bill Monroe to arrange the sound of these instruments into a bluegrass configuration, filled with complex counterpoint and jazzlike improvisations, some twenty years hence. (Significantly, Dad Blackard, leader of the string band, was the grandfather of bluegrass greats Jim and Jesse.)

But the real stars of the Bristol Sessions, the ones whose legacy would prove most influential to country music, transcending the big-city condescension to hillbilly music to become artists of the highest magnitude, were the Carter Family and Jimmie Rodgers.

The Carter Family

A. P. Carter, in many ways, was an ordinary member of the mountain community—the sort that many would deride as a hillbilly—but he researched and collected old-time folk music with the zeal of an anthropologist or a Smithsonian archivist. Carter reportedly would travel hundreds of miles, asking people to play and collecting their songs. On one of these music-lover's rambles he heard a woman singing, accompanied by an autoharp—the beautiful and talented Sara Dougherty. It was love at first sight, and they married in 1915. The music-loving couple made their living from "mostly farm related" jobs, and "usually performed for nothing more than sheer enjoyment."[7] Occasionally, churches would invite A. P. and Sara to appear in what the Carter Family's promotional handbills would later declare to be a "morally good" program of music.[8]

Before long, A. P. and Sara invited another shirttail relative to join them, Maybelle Carter (née Addington). She was the wife of A. P.'s brother Ezra; she was also Sara's cousin. Maybelle brought to the group remarkable virtuosity and innovation as a musician. She had essentially invented her own way of playing the guitar, one that opened up the possibilities of the instrument and has influenced guitar players ever since. She played the melody on the bass strings—with her thumb—while, at the same time, strumming the high strings for the rhythm. She also experimented with tuning the bass strings to different notes, according to what key the song was in. Most guitar players then, and now, either just strummed chords, laying down a rhythmic accompaniment, or picked out some melodic line. Maybelle did both at the same time, which needless to say, is very difficult to do. The techniques she pioneered have been labeled "the Carter style" by guitar aficionados. Thus, to use   • **33** rock and roll terminology, Maybelle Carter might be considered the first "guitar god."

Eventually, Maybelle's daughters were brought into the group: Helen, Anita, and June. Proving that musical gifts do indeed run in the family, these young women had great talent of their own. By this time, the Carter Family was not just a singing group, they were an act, appearing on live shows, radio, and the national stage. After A. P. and Sara left the group, Mother Maybelle and the Carter Sisters carried on and became stars at the Grand Ole Opry. June Carter, in addition to harmonizing, took on the role of the funny one. By adding jokes and acting the part of the naive country girl—à la Minnie Pearl—June's schtick helped to establish what would become a convention among country music performers. June would later marry Johnny Cash—and help bring him to Christ.

At the time of the Bristol Sessions, though, the Carter Family consisted of just A. P. (who was thirty-six years old), Sara (who was twenty-nine), and Maybelle (who was just eighteen). But everything that would make for their future success was here: A. P.'s material (both wide-ranging folk songs with ancient roots and original material in the same tradition), Maybelle's guitar, and their richly blending voices.

Sara and Maybelle were seemingly content to keep their performances confined to the family sitting room or similarly domestic and friendly environs, such as small social gatherings or church, but A. P. envisioned more for the trio. Years before the Bristol Sessions were held, Brunswick Records, having heard about this family of musicians, offered A. P. a record deal. The label stipulated, though, that he could only record his fiddle numbers and square-dance songs.

Instead of grabbing this record deal, Carter—showing the mountain integrity that so often flummoxed big-city dealers trying to offer these poverty-stricken musicians money—turned down the label's offer. The reason he gave was that the offer violated his religious beliefs.

Apparently, A. P.—though he seemed to play every kind of music under the sun—believed that playing only for dance halls would not be pleasing to the Lord. He wanted to sing about faith, family, and human emotions—what he called "heart songs." And this is what the Carter Family did at the Bristol Sessions.

From the very first song recorded by the Carter Family, "Bury Me under the Weeping Willow," all of the elements were already in place that would make the Carters a lasting sensation: the harmony of Sara and Maybelle, with A. P. "bassing in"—as his sporadic low harmony came to be called—for most of the verses and especially on the chorus; the single line guitar work of Maybelle heard on two separate breaks; and the lyrics of this centuries-old folk ballad about a rejected woman dying for love—with its vivid imagery of emotional devastation, death, and burial—presented with empathy and authenticity.

"The Little Log Cabin by the Sea" may be the location sung about in another Carter Family song, but it is the "precious, precious Bible" that is its heart. The verses are all about a Bible given to the singer by her mother. Read your Bible is the message here, which "tells me how to live and how to die"—a true exhortation concerning the words of the Lord, placed against the backdrop of mother, home, and the cabin by the sea. The song exhibits fine harmony, and Maybelle's guitar is again given two distinctive showcases.

Maybe the strongest of the Bristol recordings of the Carter Family is "The Poor Orphan Child." Most songs with this sort of title, such as "The Blind Child" or "The Little Paper Boy," are ballads, emotional laments over the fate of the song's title character. Here, however, the vocalists offer a rousing number, in which the Savior is asked to lead the orphan by the hand and walk in glory towards God. This is an exhilarating, almost marching song of affirmation concerning Christ's ability to take care of the poor and the bereft. Nearly seventy years later, Gillian Welch would reprise the imagery of this song in her "Orphan Girl," which asks the Savior to take the part of her father, mother, brother, and sister until she can be with them in heaven.

"The Wandering Boy" is probably the least distinctive of the Carters' Bristol songs. A. P. is not present, and the vocal is a solo by Sara. It is a plea for the return of a woman's errant son;

the theme seems in line with a Carter Family record, but lacking any harmony, the sound is unusually thin.

The identical instrumentation and vocal solo found on "The Wandering Boy" is also present in "Single Girl, Married Girl"—a superior and more forceful performance in which Sara sings straightforward advice to single girls about the potentially unglamorous situations of a youthful wife's marriage. What distinguishes the song is the strong guitar line from Maybelle and the more interesting commentary: "Single girl, single girl, going dressed fine;/Married girl, married girl, wears just anything. . . . Single girl, single girl, goes to the store and buys;/Married girl, married girl, rocks the cradle and cries. . . . Single girl, single girl, she's going where she please;/Married girl, married girl, baby on her knees." This song depicts an unromanticized and clear-eyed account of the differences between single and married life, between freedom and responsibility. For all of their songs that celebrate motherhood, this one shows a tough-minded sense of humor about the subject. It also anticipates the tough-minded marriage songs of Loretta Lynn, Tammy Wynette, and other female country singers to come, who honestly face up to how "sometimes it's hard to be a woman," while still affirming the institutions of marriage and motherhood.

The Carter Family may have been known for their heart songs of home and hearth, but—like much of the country music they engendered—they balanced any tendencies towards sentimentality with this kind of stark realism. Years after the Bristol Sessions, when they had become national stars, their signature tune was "Keep on the Sunny Side," an original composition by A. P. The title makes it sound like a paean to sunny optimism. Indeed, that is what the chorus amounts to. But each verse is filled with darkness and gloom. The opening verse sets up two patterns of imagery and two facets of life:

> There's a dark and a troubled side of life;
> There's a bright and sunny side too;
> Though we meet with the darkness and strife,
> The sunny side may also find you.

The bright side is clearly the afterthought. The imagery of darkness, trouble, and strife overwhelms the more summarily stated "bright and sunny side." The next verse has the storms of life blowing our hopes away—though afterward there is a little sun. The only ground for optimism is faith: "Let us trust in our Savior always/Who keepeth us in His care."

In their song that became even more famous, "Will the Circle Be Unbroken" (credited to A. P., though it exists in other versions), the poignant miseries of life are resolved "bye and bye," in the grand reunion of heaven. Until then, this world is a vale of tears. Again, each verse is heartbreaking:

> I was standin' by my window
> On one cold and cloudy day,
> When I saw this hearse come rollin'
> For to carry my mother away.
>
> Lord, I told the undertaker,
> "Undertaker, please drive slow,
> For this body you are haulin'
> Lord, I hate to see her go."
>
> I will follow close behind her,
> Try to hold off and be brave,
> But I could not hide my sorrow
> When they laid her in the grave.

The stanzas constitute an achingly sad funeral song, the poignancy accented by the homely language. But after each verse is the exuberantly affirmative chorus of faith:

> Will the circle be unbroken?
> Bye and bye, Lord, bye and bye;
> There's a better home a-waitin',
> In the sky, Lord, in the sky.

The family circle—when everyone would sit around the parlor facing each other to sing—will be restored, unbroken, in the consummation of everlasting life. The whole song, including the bleak emotions, constitutes a prayer addressed to the Lord. •37

The Carters, who sing so much about home (and about mothers) here look ahead to a better home.

Jimmie Rodgers

The day job of the Carter Family was working on the farm—to be specific, they sold tree cuttings. Jimmie Rodgers worked on the railroad and became known by the stage moniker "the Singing Brakeman." Thus, one could say that the Carter Family came out of rural America, while Rodgers represented newly industrial America. The Carters sang about wildwood flowers, log cabins, and mountain culture. Rodgers, for all the claims of his fathering country, sang about trains, cities, and skid rows. The Carters sang about and seemed to exemplify family values. Rodgers sang about drinking, womanizing, and razor fights—in the words of one of his songs, "my rough and rowdy ways." Ever since, country music has exhibited both extremes.

And yet, as much as one might want to make the clear-cut distinction that the Carter Family represented the values and the heart of rural America while Jimmie Rodgers represented the bad side of the tracks, the equation refuses to break down with such simplicity. Not only did the Carters sing about the dark and troubled side of life, as we have seen, their family circle was indeed broken. Sara and A. P.'s marriage was a troubled one, and they divorced in 1939. (Even after their marriage broke up, they still performed together until 1943. Maybelle and her daughters kept performing as Mother Maybelle and the Carter Sisters, becoming stars at the Grand Ole Opry and even touring with Elvis Presley in 1956. At Maybelle's urging, A. P. and Sara came back to the group, and the Carter Family was reunited from 1952 to 1956.)

Conversely, Jimmie Rodgers, for all of his rough and rowdy ways, sang songs of nostalgia and yearning for a family life he hardly knew. Both the Carter Family and Rodgers depicted, in a realistic and honest way, what they knew of the human condition.

More so than the other performers who debuted on *The Bristol Sessions*, Jimmie Rodgers and The Carter Family lived the songs they sang, or so it surely seemed to all who heard them. Jimmie's songs of being a rounder and the Carters' lament to a young wife struck an inner chord in the listener and had a type of authority not found in earlier recorded performances, setting a strong precedent for the music to come.

Before the Bristol Sessions, Rodgers had been singing regularly on a low-power radio station in Asheville, North Carolina, backed by an already formed string band trio, the Teneva Ramblers. The evening before the recording session, however, the band had an argument with Jimmie over the group's billing. The Teneva Ramblers left Rodgers and recorded "The Longest Train I Ever Saw" for Peer under their own name. For his part, Rodgers found himself in Bristol, on the night before his chance to record, without any accompanying musicians.

Rodgers' ability to rise above the circumstances showed the performer's self-confidence (real or bluffed). He persuaded Ralph Peer to record him as a solo performer, accompanied only by his guitar. The Ramblers' refusal to perform with Rodgers worked to his advantage, as his first record showcased Jimmie's plaintive and mournful voice in "The Soldier's Sweetheart," with no string band backing to distract from the purity and unique timbre of his voice. With limited guitar skills, Rodgers' later recordings would continue to feature his voice as his primary, or most captivating, instrument.

Not that his voice was notable for its musicality; rather, Rodgers had a rough, loose, natural sort of singing voice, more like Bob Dylan than Nelson Eddy. (In fact, there is evidence that Dylan purposefully imitated Rodgers, as well as other early performers.) What made Rodgers' singing so appealing was its sense of authenticity, the way he could connect with listeners and communicate with them, seemingly person to person, common man to common man. If Rodgers is the father of country music, it is surely because of this precedent. Ever since, the human voice has been the most important quality of a country music performer. This does not downplay the importance of instrumental skills, but for the most part it is the voice—not so much its melodiousness but the sense of sincerity, authenticity, and personality—that makes a record work as country.

Rodgers only recorded two songs at the Bristol Sessions. With his former group, he had been singing newer-sounding pop songs, which he thought to play for the record company, but Peer asked him to sing some older ones—as Charles Wolfe put it, "ones that sounded old but could be copyrighted."[9]

Jimmie recorded "The Soldier's Sweetheart" (a World War I song), to the tune of the old Irish ballad "The River Shannon." He also did an old lullaby "Sleep, Baby, Sleep," tying into the popular mother motif and featuring his trademark yodel. "I thought his yodel alone might spell success,"[10] Peer remarked, so these two tunes were released on a 78 rpm record.

Rodgers soon became savvy to the show business necessity of self-promotion and seized opportunities. Late in Sara Carter's life, when she was asked what the Carter Family did immediately following their trip to Bristol, she said, "We went home and planted corn." Life went back to normal, if it had ever deviated. Farming and occasional local performances continued to make up the lives of A. P., Sara, and Maybelle. But Jimmie Rodgers planted seeds of a different sort, for when he learned of Victor Records' release date for his two songs, he took action. Rodgers did what would today be called putting on a front. He traveled to New York, home of Victor Records and Ralph Peer, and checked into a classy hotel. From there he called Peer, asking when he should come by to make some more records. Whether bluff, optimism, or desperation, the plan worked. Rodgers recorded four more songs under the guidance of Peer in late November 1927. With releasable songs in the Victor vaults and his first record starting to sell, Rodgers' career had begun.

This single incident of self-promotion demonstrates Rodgers' awareness of the ways of the world. Unlike A. P. Carter, Rodgers seemed to know something about creating an image.[11] He began using the railroad worker as a persona, associating himself with the ways and lifestyle of a rambler. He was very conscious of his image, and once the public became aware of Rodgers, they became aware of a very particular and well-cultivated image—this, in the days before the existence of the star-making machinery of the major labels.

In fact, Rodgers would have three well-defined personas, all overlapping and, surprisingly, not confusing or competing with one another. He was first known as the Singing Brakeman. Then, as more and more records featuring his trademark yodels were issued, he became equally well known as America's Blue Yodeler. Finally, after his death, Rodgers was heralded as the father of country music. As such, he engendered not just a style of music but the country music industry itself, in all of its later showbiz manipulations.

With his varied background, Rogers certainly could have sold himself as a variety of things. And the role of a railroad man was not a fabrication. But Rodgers seemed to sense the potential appeal of this image over that of many of his other itinerant professions. As country music scholar Bill Malone points out in his book of transcribed speeches on early country music, the image of the cowboy was far preferable and more romantic for a performer (and an audience) to embrace than that of the hillbilly.[12] Like the freedom represented by the cowboy, the life of the itinerant boxcar-jumping brakeman undoubtedly suited Rodgers' self-created public persona and was more to his liking than that of a farmer. The public wanted escape, and Rodgers' image suggested the freedom of the rails, the traveling man with no strings to tie him down, a life lived outside the norm.

Although songs of faithless lovers were not new to either popular song or hillbilly music when Rodgers began to record, the attitude that Rodgers brought to such vignettes seemed different. He presented a cocksure, clear-eyed stance that exuded confidence. Also, Rodgers seemed slightly amused at the proceedings, which sounded as if they were very close to his personal situation—or so he would have us believe.

The world Rodgers sang about was not the middle-class parlor but the poolroom, the speakeasy (in a time of prohibition), the gambling den, and the wrong side of the tracks over by the railyard. He sang about confrontations with the "po-leece" and rendered bemused reflections about being "In the Jailhouse Now." In one of his signature songs, "Blue Yodel #1" ("T for Texas"), the imagery makes today's gangster-rappers seem tame. After singing how T is not only for Texas, it's for Thelma, "the

gal that made a wreck out of me," he takes his complaint a step
further:

> I'm goin' buy me a pistol, just as long as I'm tall;
> Goin' to buy me a pistol, just as long as I'm tall;
> I'm gonna shoot poor Thelma,
> Just to see her jump and fall.

And once that's done, "I'm goin' buy me a shotgun, with a great
long shiny barrel," so that he can "shoot that rounder that stole
away my girl."

Rodgers often seems cavalier, almost as if condoning the
actions being portrayed in his songs. There had always been
murder ballads and songs about adultery, vice, and rounders.
But usually there was at least a veneer of moral instruction.
Though such songs undoubtedly owed their popularity to their
titillating subject matter, they were usually presented as cautionary tales, with sentiments about how sad the situation was
and how we should strive to be better. Instead, Rodgers tells
them in an engaging manner, so that they appear humorous,
but also what would later be described as cool.

When Rodgers, in one of his most famous songs, sings about
Frankie shooting Johnnie three times through the door, describing the shots as "rootie-toot toot," there is a certain glee in
Rodgers' voice. This song overtly tells the listener that this is
not a sermon on how to behave but just a picture "from life's
other side," as Hank Williams might say. Rodgers explains at
the song's end that there is no message here and certainly no
moral for the listener to take away. Instead, it is merely an example that "there ain't no good in men." It is not clear whether he
is expounding on or reveling in the doctrine of total depravity.

Rodgers did not write "Frankie and Johnny." He did, however, compose many of his own songs, and near the middle of
his career he began to write autobiographical numbers. Naturally, a songwriter is not committed to present an accurate self-
image or even a single or unified point of view in his or her
work. But Rodgers placed himself into a few of his songs in

such a way that it is difficult to believe that they did not reflect his actual life.

In "Jimmie the Kid," he calls himself by name and then relates his railroad-to-riches life. In "My Rough and Rowdy Ways," he is outright confessional: "For years and years I rambled, drank my wine and gambled," he sings, but then he met a real lady and settled down, corresponding perhaps to his own marriage. "But I cannot forget my old rambling ways"—especially when he hears a railroad train. He'll go down to the poolroom. Get a drink. As in the great American novels from *Huckleberry Finn* to those of Hemingway, the song speaks of a man's inner rebellion against the restraints of domesticity. This confessional quality, the sense (genuine or illusory) of a real human being pouring out his or her heart with blunt honesty, would also become a prized quality in country music, from the soap opera lives of Tammy Wynette and George Jones to the searing introspections of Merle Haggard.

Part of the subversive quality of Rodgers' songs, in the 1930s, must have been his flirtation, as a Southern white man, with black culture. His blue yodels, combining twelve-bar blues with his inimitable yodel—a combination that may seem unpromising but works incredibly well—often sound as if they would be more at home in a Harlem speakeasy than at a country music gathering. And though Rodgers most often sang with just his unaccompanied guitar, his blue yodels were often backed by languid horns playing Dixieland-style jazz. To this day, some country purists deny Rodgers' role in country music. Longtime Grand Ole Opry member Charlie Louvin speaks with unhidden disdain about Rodgers' title as the father of country music. "I don't see how anybody can call him that," Louvin argues. "He had horns on his records—isn't that supposed to be the worst thing possible?" Others think the irritation some have about Rodgers' reputation goes deeper. Music scholar James Walsh reacts quickly when told that some older country musicians reject Rodgers' importance. "It's because he played with blacks," flatly states Walsh. Indeed, Rodgers recorded "Blue Yodel #9" with a young Louis Armstrong on trumpet and Mrs. Armstrong sitting in on the ragtime-sounding piano.

For all of Rodgers' image as a rounder, it would be wrong to assume that all of his songs were rough and rowdy. Rodgers' recorded output actually leans surprisingly close to the themes sung about by the Carter Family. A good illustration of this phenomenon is Webb Pierce, the great country star of a later era. While hard drinking songs usually come to mind when one mentions Pierce, in truth the man had only one hit song that celebrated alcohol, out of more than a dozen Top 10 hits. But because his 1951 hit "There Stands the Glass" was so powerfully memorable, it forever associated Webb Pierce with drinking songs.[13] The same is true, to a different extent, with Jimmie Rodgers. There were really only a handful of his songs that raised eyebrows, but fed by legend and hit records, the image of Rodgers as a train-jumping free spirit became an indelible image in the minds of Americans between the wars.

Some of his best music consisted of beautiful—and innocent—love songs: "Mississippi Moon," "The One Rose," "My Blue-Eyed Jane." And he arguably outdid the Carters when it came to writing and singing sentimental songs about mothers. As early as his first recording session after Bristol, in November 1927, Rodgers was singing heart songs, such as "Mother Was a Lady." Sometimes his rough and rowdy persona clashes with the sentimental mother's boy persona, in ways that are often unintentionally humorous. "Mother, the Queen of My Heart" is a ballad that begins with a mother sending off her boy, making him promise that he will never gamble. Whereupon the lad becomes a professional gambler. Many wasted years later, he is in a big card game. He bets everything he has, to draw for a royal flush. He gets the card: it's exactly the one he needs, the Queen of Hearts. But as he looks at that card, it reminds him of his mother—"the Queen of My Heart"—and his broken promises to her. He throws down his hand, losing everything, in an act of repentance and mother love.

It would be wrong to think such sentiments—however over the top in this case—were not deeply sincere. In addition to all of his mother tributes, many of which were in fictional contexts, Rodgers recorded two heartfelt tributes to his father, in "My Old Pal" and "Daddy and Home."

Such family themes resurfaced with particular strength early in 1932 when Rodgers recorded a song he wrote called "Down the Old Road to Home," in which he yearns for home and family. The next day as the recording session continued, Rodgers seemed to bring closure to this lament with "Home Call," in which he sings of domestic bliss, mentioning his wife and daughter by name, happy with the simplicity of being at home with "Carrie, Anita, and me." Not since "Jimmie the Kid" had Rodgers been so specifically autobiographical.

Even before his recording career began, Rodgers was plagued by tuberculosis. In fact, his poor health seems to have been what caused him to quit the railroads and to start a musical career instead. In January of 1931, Rodgers recorded "T.B. Blues," in which he recounts his fatalistic attitude toward the disease. He begins the song by explaining how he gets angry with his "good gal" for trying to cheer him up and convince him that he really doesn't have T.B. He says she is making a fool of him with this optimism. He also sings of being in a rain of sorrow and says that, even though he is fighting like a lion, nobody has ever whipped the disease and so he too will die. The song ends with Rodgers imagining the loneliness of the graveyard, with mud being thrown down onto his face. There is no light here, and the song strays close to self-pity—an emotion rarely associated with Rodgers.

In August of 1932, Rodgers returned to the topic with "Whippin' That Old T.B." And while his good gal may not have convinced Jimmie that he was a well man, Rodgers shows a very changed attitude here. Even the title of the song declares the change, from having the blues to defeating the disease. With the optimism of a true zealot, he begins the song by urging others in his situation to take encouragement from his example, and "don't worry about consumption," even if it's diagnosed as T.B. He happily dismisses the gloomy prognosis of his physicians, saying that "happiness and sunshine" are what has done him the most good. Also true to form, the singer unhesitatingly admits that some of his "happiness" stems from his consumption of alcohol. "Don't let the T.B. get you down," he again admonishes fellow sufferers near the end of the song and then • **45** makes a joke out of dying by advising everyone to live, since "nine out of ten" people won't care if you die anyway.

Despite this bit of positive thinking, he was fading fast. Ten months later, desperately ill, he went to the studios of Victor Records in New York for one more recording session. It is said that he wanted to provide additional income for his wife before he died. The label supplied a bed so that he could rest between takes. He had to perform sitting down. He recorded twelve titles in eight days. The studio had provided musicians to back him up, but on his last recording, "Years Ago," he insisted on playing alone, with only his guitar for accompaniment, just as he had done at the Bristol Sessions. Thirty-six hours later, on May 26, 1933, he died.

He was thirty-six years old. His career lasted six years. This was another country music convention he unintentionally fathered: the brilliant but doomed artist—like Hank Williams, Patsy Cline, Keith Whitley, and Elvis Presley—who died tragically and too young.

Jimmie Rodgers recorded only one gospel song, a number he cowrote with Elsie McWilliams entitled "The Wonderful City." It was recorded in 1931 as a duet with Sara Carter.

> I'm waiting, watching and longing
> That beautiful sight to behold
> When I shall awake some bright morning
> In that city of streets of pure gold;
>
> My Saviour has gone to prepare it
> For all who accept His grace
> And that's why I know I'll be welcome
> To a home in that wonderful place.

Who knows what Rodgers contributed to this song and whether the faith it professes was really his? But this urban railroad man makes a point sometimes forgotten by country folk who idealize rural life and are repelled by the evils of the big city. Heaven, in fact, is a big city.

4

Nashville

FROM THE OPRY TO THE OUTLAWS

After the Bristol Sessions, it did not take long for country music to become an acquired taste, an industry, and an institution. The new technologies of the phonograph and the radio spread the sound coast to coast. Big money could be made from hit records, by both backwoods artists and slick studios. Radio stations were not just playing records, though; they were broadcasting live performances from local stations, often giving local talent a shot at the big time.

Country music began as regional music, reflecting the folk cultures of the white working classes, not only in the South but in the West. Technically, the term is "country and western" music. This included not only cowboy music (particularly, its Hollywood redactions) but also western swing, one of the great musical innovations in American culture. In Texas and Oklahoma, Bob Wills and his imitators had fused the big band sound—with its wind instruments and jazz stylings—with a distinctly western and country sound. As the Depression sent thousands of Dust Bowl farmers west to the promised land of California, they took their music with them. Bakersfield, California—which linguists say features exactly the same regional dialect as Oklahoma City—became another center of country and western music. And it was Bakersfield musicians, such as Buck Owens, who pioneered country music's presence in a new technology—television. It was another Bakersfield musician, Merle Haggard, who would take country music to new heights, as well as serve as a cultural lightning rod in the turmoil of the 1960s.

But it was Nashville that became the capital of country music. This was where the recording studios evolved, where the publishing companies and the agents and the impresarios were. Nashville, for better or worse, became the center of the country music business.

As country music became institutionalized, folk traditions became less important than the personal artistry of singers and songwriters. Country music began to reflect the changes in American society, both in conforming to cultural trends and in reacting against them.

The Grand Ole Opry and Tootsie's Orchid Lounge

Perhaps the most important institution in country music is the Grand Ole Opry, which is both a radio show and a live concert, in which the top acts of country music—past, present, and up-and-coming—take turns doing a couple of numbers every Saturday night. Beginning in 1925—actually two years before the Bristol Sessions—the show continues to this day. The Grand Ole Opry became a part of the golden age of radio and introduced country and western music to a national audience. It also helped to establish Nashville as the country music mecca. The Opry enforced strict standards, both musically and morally, that still influence the values of country music.

Some country music had appeared on Nashville's WSM radio station from the time it first went on the air in September 1925. But it was the hiring of George D. Hay that fall that would be the turning point. Hay had previously worked in Chicago and had been involved with starting Chicago radio's *National Barn Dance* on WLS in 1924. Hay tested the waters at the new WSM with some popular local acts, including Uncle Dave Macon (featured on *The Bristol Sessions*) and fiddler Dr. Humphrey Bate. It was the appearance of elderly fiddler Uncle Jimmy Thompson, however, that caused the greatest audience reaction (by cards and letters). On December 28, 1925, the first regularly scheduled *Barn Dance* program aired on WSM.

This radio show featured backwoods talent a full two years before the Bristol Sessions—one could make the case that the modern genre of country music had its true birth through radio. But the Bristol Sessions have a claim to fame because it launched both the country music record business and the careers of country's first national stars, Jimmie Rodgers and the Carter Family. Actually, country's twin origins are evident in the industry today, as country radio exerts a huge influence on record sales, often to the consternation of veteran and cutting-edge performers, who find themselves shut out of airplay, and thus record sales, in favor of the latest generic hat act.

By mid-1926, Hay had a stable of approximately twenty acts, whose appearances he rotated on the weekly program. It was Hay who was responsible for instituting the agrarian setting of the program, reportedly insisting that his performers wear the dungarees and overalls that would come to epitomize country music for decades to come. He was also known for telling the performers to keep things "down to earth" if the music became too complex or strayed from a traditional sound. Hay emphasized the down-home approach to the performers, many of whom he renamed with condescending agrarian titles such as The Possum Hunters, The Fruit Jar Drinkers (as in moonshine whiskey), and The Gully Jumpers. This was hillbilly music. Its appeal was often as a novelty act, an occasion to laugh at one's social inferiors.

In time, though, the creativity of country music's performers and its integrity as an art form unto itself became clearer. The term "hillbilly music" began to be challenged as derogatory. Ernest Tubb suggested the term "country and western," acknowledging the music's agrarian roots in a more neutral way. Country performers had always been self-deprecating, often accepting the hillbilly-hick role with good humor, though one might wish they had not. At a time when it would be insensitive to ridicule other social groups, poor rural Southerners were still fair game as "rednecks" and "white trash." And yet they didn't seem to mind much. The hillbilly image was played on as late as the television show *Hee Haw*, which ran from 1969 to 1993. Buck Owens, a fixture on the show—with its corny jokes, barnyard stereotypes, and lazy no-accounts sleeping with their shotguns on the porch—recently commented that he finally got tired of having to make fun of himself all the time.

Country music's assertion of its distinct identity from other styles of music was signaled (though in a characteristically jocular way) in May 1927, when the *Barn Dance* was christened with a new name. The program followed the NBC network broadcast of the Metropolitan Opera from New York City. George D. Hay, serving as the announcer, quipped that listeners had just heard the Grand Opera. But now they were going to hear "the Grand Ole Opry." The joke and the name stuck.

Before long, the Grand Ole Opry had become an institution. The Nashville radio station WSM was a "clear channel" broadcaster, which meant it had an unusually powerful radio beam, with no competing stations on its frequency. People from across the forty-eight states could tune to 650 AM and, if the skies were clear, pick up Nashville's WSM and listen to the Opry.

Soon NBC syndicated a half-hour segment of the three-hour show, making it a national program in the golden age of radio. Performers lucky enough to get scheduled for that particular segment, sponsored by Prince Albert Tobacco, thus gained national exposure and a shot at tremendous record sales. Charlie Louvin has said that this reduced the number of gospel songs on the Opry, since it was felt that hard-core Christian songs wouldn't go over well being sponsored by a tobacco company.

In the 1920s, the show was made up of largely amateur, or semiprofessional musicians. Big names included the Crook Brothers, the Binkley Brothers, and DeFord Bailey. Bailey is of special note because he was a black performer. It is said that he was told never to speak on the air, but only to play his instrument. Bailey was on the Opry for many years, but was later dropped and ignored. Understandably bitter, Bailey was later persuaded by the great country star Roy Acuff to return to the stage for his proper due at a reunion broadcast.

As country music turned into a veritable entertainment industry, stars were born. The Carter Family became Opry regulars. Ernest Tubb, who began as a Jimmie Rodgers disciple but later forged a distinct sound of his own, moved from Texas to Nashville to become a member of the Grand Ole Opry. It was a distinct honor to be made a member of the Opry—a regular performer. Members were obligated to make regular appearances and were paid at scale, no matter how much they made in their concerts and record deals. Even though the biggest stars could make far more money doing concerts on their own, they generally considered being a member of the Grand Ole Opry the height of their professional achievement and continued to make the required number of appearances every year.

Country music became more sophisticated. Eddy Arnold began his career as "the Tennessee Plowboy" with a hard-edged country band, but he developed into a smooth-voiced crooner. "Bouquet of Roses," "I'll Hold You in My Heart (till I Can Hold You in My Arms)," and "Anytime" were some of the hits that made him country music radio's most successful artist of the twentieth century, in terms of number one singles. Other great vocal stylists given prominence by the Opry included Ray Price, Jim Reeves, and Patsy Cline.

Ernest Tubb was the second most popular radio performer of the 1940s (behind Arnold) according to *Billboard Magazine*. His hits were many, and his fans were devoted. Ernest Tubb showed respect for country's past (by persuading RCA Victor to rerelease the records of his idol, Jimmie Rodgers, for example), while simultaneously forging country's future by constantly encouraging and fostering new talent. Known as a tireless promoter of country music as a legitimate art form (as opposed to just hillbilly music), Tubb was responsible for helping a great number of struggling performers get recognition and, often, get onto the stage of the Opry itself. This was certainly true late in the decade with the likes of Hank Snow and Hank Williams.

A particularly important presence on the Opry was Roy Acuff. Originally a professional baseball player, he turned his full attention to music when he was permanently benched due to sunstroke. He started out as Roy Acuff and His Crazy Tennesseans recording semirisqué music. But he toned down his act to land a job with the Grand Ole Opry. He became famous for his fiddle playing and for his strong, twangy country voice, which specialized in gospel numbers. "The Great Speckled Bird" and "The Precious Jewel" are two of Acuff's most enduring numbers. Acuff was not only a fine performer, he was—for all of his down-home image—a canny businessman. Together with the early recording impresario Fred Rose, Acuff formed a publishing company that practically cornered the market in the country music publishing business. To this day, the Acuff Rose company is still a major copyright holder and music publisher in Nashville and beyond. Acuff was a major player in the growth of country music as big business.

As George D. Hay presided over the Opry, he became known as "the solemn old judge." He insisted that all of the performances follow standards of strict moral propriety. For example, he did not allow songs about alcohol, a prohibition that lasted long after he left the show. Once, Hank Williams wanted to perform his hit "My Bucket's Got a Hole in It," a novelty song about buckets of beer. On the Opry stage, he changed the lyrics to refer to buckets of milk. Hay wanted country music to uphold traditional values as well as traditional sounds. (As to the latter, he forbade horns, drums, and electric instruments—prohibitions that were later lifted after Hay was gone.)[1] He wanted the music to be wholesome, suitable for the whole family, and a good influence on its listeners.

In fact, the Opry began to be staged in what was once a church. The Ryman Auditorium was originally constructed as a church building. It retained its stained glass windows, and the multitudes of Opry-goers—for whom the show was not just a radio program but a weekly concert—sat in pews. The Ryman was called the mother church of country music, and the values it projected were self-consciously in harmony with those taught in real churches.

Behind the Ryman, though, across the alley, is Tootsie's Orchid Lounge. Opry performers waiting to go onstage would often sneak out the back of the Ryman, dash across the alley, and slip through the back door into Tootsie's—the quintessential country bar, with its hard liquor, honky-tonk angels, and guitar singers playing for tips. In its smoky haze, country stars would drink until someone came to fetch them when it was their turn to go on. Then they would dash back to the wholesome venue of the Opry.

The Ryman and Tootsie's represent the two poles of country music, which had its origins in both the church and the honky-tonk, has always been both conservative and wild, and has always consisted of artists who drew upon both traditional values and their own self-destructive impulses. Just as symbolic is the alley between the two. It isn't that country music performers would line up on one side or the other of this moral divide. Rather, a single performer would run back and forth between them and was equally at home in both worlds.

Though the performers often made jokes about the "solemn old judge's" restrictions and ran off to Tootsie's every chance they got, there is little reason to think that they would have changed what the Opry stood for. They usually shared these values, even though they might not have lived up to them. The widespread respect and veneration for the Opry among country music performers has always included an appreciation for the values it represents. This family-friendly tradition in country music is still influential today. "I'll never record anything that could not be performed on the Grand Ole Opry," says Brad Paisley, a contemporary singer-songwriter. "I think you know what I mean. They've gotten a little more lenient, and that's fine. But I wouldn't feel comfortable letting down the folks that attend the Grand Ole Opry."[2]

By the mid-1930s, Hay had lost control of the program. In part, he was a victim of the show's success and its place in the ever-growing financial empire of the Nashville music industry. First, he was eased out by the businessmen WSM had hired to book tours for the increasing number of acts that regularly appeared on the show. The tours were set up as a symbiotic relationship in which the acts would promote the show, and the radio program would promote the acts. Because of the money involved in tours and promotion, Hay's role as program stage manager and broadcast organizer took a backseat to the business of music and economics. Additionally, Hay's health began to fail, and he was absent from the day-to-day workings of the show sometimes for months at a time. By 1938, George D. Hay's role with the program and his power had been severely diminished.

The Grand Ole Opry continued to grow in power and prestige through the 1950s. There were other country music programs on the air, but the Opry had pride of place and was by far the most influential. For while *Louisiana Hayride* and *Ozark Jubilee,* among others, were offering live weekend broadcasts of country music, these were often seen as minor league training grounds for performers with their sights set on the Opry stage. Some, like Lefty Frizzell and Hank Thompson, chose to leave the Opry after a short time, finding the strictly enforced rules too confining. But most artists were willing to accept these restrictions for a chance to perform on the Opry.

The biggest change—again reflecting what the country music industry had become—took place in 1974 when the show moved out of the venerable Ryman Auditorium into a theme park. Opryland featured rides and games and a glitzy resort, all centered around a larger concert hall built to pack in the increasing number of tourists flooding to Nashville to see the Opry. A big corporate venture, Opryland became part of an entertainment empire that included cable TV channels The Nashville Network (TNN) and Country Music Television (CMT), as videos had begun to replace the radio as the medium of choice for popular music. Later, in the merger-mania of the nineties, the whole conglomeration was bought by media giant Viacom, which also owned CBS and MTV, shifting the center of power from Nashville to New York City.

But through all the changes, the Opry itself has remained much the same. Unlike flavor-of-the-week pop stars, who are dropped by studios and fans as soon as their five minutes of fame are up, the Grand Ole Opry reveres its older performers. Hank Snow and Grandpa Jones continued to perform at the Opry right up to the time of their deaths, and great performers of the past—now old men and old women—keep singing, alongside recent superstars and brand-new talent. WSM still broadcasts the show over clear channel, and a half-hour sample—as in the golden age of radio—can be seen every week on TNN. To be at the Opry in person, for a three-hour show that features over twenty classic and contemporary performers, is still one of the best concert experiences in America.

The Times They Are a-Changing

By the end of World War II, country music was flourishing. After the cataclysm of a world war, the struggle against fascism, and the new, fearful specter of communism, Americans were treasuring their heritage—and country and western music felt like American music.

The 1940s were a good time artistically as well. There was as yet no attempt to make all of the music sound the same for the benefit of radio programmers. The performers could develop their own styles, and if their work found an audience it would also find its way to radio and records. Vocalists, instrumentalists, small groups and large, were all making contributions to the country music world of the 1940s.

In many ways, the 1950s were the defining decade for country music. It turned major corners, for better or worse, and enjoyed a national popularity that had been building steadily for years. During this decade such artists as Bill Monroe, Chet Atkins, and Hank Snow were all at their peaks, offering country music audiences some of their most memorable performances. The Louvin Brothers demonstrated what close harmony could do. The twin stars of Lefty Frizzell and Hank Williams burned brightly (before they burned themselves out). Ray Price, onetime roommate of Hank Williams, hired Hank's band, The Drifting Cowboys, after Williams' death, purposefully (and successfully) sounding very much like the dead star—but he soon found a sound of his own as a rich-voiced country crooner. Growing musical sophistication led also to the rise of the crossover sensation Patsy Cline, who dazzled not only country fans but pop fans as well, with her stunning voice and her expressive style.

Bill Monroe invented bluegrass, which was, in effect, a new musical genre, combining the oldest and most traditional tunes with virtuoso instrumental improvisations. In his train followed a host of new artists exploring the genre. Lester Flatt and Earl Scruggs left Bill Monroe's band late in the decade, releasing in 1958 a banjo-driven collection of largely traditional songs that would soon place them more firmly in the consciousness of middle America than Monroe would ever be. The Stanley Brothers also became hugely popular with their own take on Monroe's style of music.

Instrumental proficiency was prized during the fifties. Chet Atkins sold a huge number of records as a solo guitarist. Atkins also became a creative record producer, experimenting with what would become known as the Nashville sound, bringing in orchestral strings as well as steel guitars. As a producer, Atkins was also responsible for turning former hillbilly singer Jim Reeves into a velvety-voiced stylist.

Patriotism reigned in country music. The Korean War was a galvanizing force for country music, more so than for other forms of pop music. Numbers such as "From a Mother's Arms to Korea" and "There's a Star-Spangled Banner Waving Somewhere" were both topical and patriotic. Earlier, country music had dealt with World War II in Ernest Tubb's "Soldier's Last Letter" and Gene Autry's "At Mail Call Today," from 1944 and 1945, respectively. And although these songs were written about World War II, they were just as relevant a few years later for the Korean conflict, as were the Louvin Brothers' "Weapon of Prayer" and "Searching for a Soldier's Grave."

The country music community of the fifties was not oblivious to politics. Roy Acuff twice ran for governor. Songs like "Don't Take the Flag Out of Our Classroom," recorded by several artists, made their point. The Cold War was addressed by the great Hank Williams, who recorded (as Luke the Drifter) "No, No Joe." While "the Flag" was sung in deadly earnest, Williams is more relaxed and self-assured in his condemnation of Joe Stalin, making fun of the Communist dictator's inability to get a foothold in the United States.

The 1950s saw country music apparently satisfied with itself. It was pure and recognizable in sound and had a clearly defined audience. Performers strove for an individual sound, but didn't seem to worry if they sounded like each other. But then came Elvis.

As much as any other social force, be it the Korean War or the McCarthy hearings, the emergence of Elvis Presley was critical to the decade. Elvis hit nationally with "Heartbreak Hotel" on RCA Records in 1956. But before this breakthrough, he labored in the Sun Studios of Memphis with producer Sam Phillips, creating and honing a sound.

He was essentially—at least at the beginning—a country singer. Recording at the same time at Sun Studios were the recognizably country Johnny Cash, Carl Perkins, and Jerry Lee Lewis, who were experimenting with a rockabilly sound, taking hillbilly music and combining it with the African-American sound of rhythm and blues. Elvis was very much a country performer in his repertoire and sensibility. So it was natural that he was invited to perform at the Grand Ole Opry.

By all accounts, Elvis was treated politely if not enthusiastically by the Opry members and the audience, though some thought his appearance—with his long sideburns—rather strange. When Elvis visited the Opry for his sole performance there, he was reportedly nervous about running into the great Bill Monroe. This was because Elvis, showing his country music taste, had just released a cover of Monroe's bluegrass number "Blue Moon of Kentucky." Elvis admired him and was afraid that Monroe would see Presley's livelier new arrangement as sacrilege or disrespect. But when the two met at the Opry, Monroe said how much he liked the new version. In fact, when Monroe recorded "Blue Moon of Kentucky" again, he followed Elvis' up-tempo interpretation.

But when Elvis became a phenomenon, the shock waves in country music were unmistakable. Country music did not cease to exist, as some feared, but many performers—even popular and established artists—had to take a hard look at what they were doing if they planned to remain viable recording and performing acts. Record sales began to be dominated by rock and roll. Country music started losing its market share, as more and more radio stations dropped country for the new, hipper music. Perhaps the most symbolic microcosm was when WLS in Chicago changed their format from country music and agrarian information to straight-ahead Top 40 rock. The pioneering WLS *Barn Dance*, which had preceded even the Grand Ole Opry, gave way to the prerecorded sounds of pop music's British Invasion.

This new rock and roll, though partially rooted in country music, was somehow just too different. It could not be contained simply as another genre within the larger realm of country music, as with Bill Monroe's bluegrass or Bob Wills' western swing. This was something new, and as it became increasingly popular both on radio stations and with the record-buying public, country music felt threatened. Ernest Tubb mused whether he should even remain in the business or go sell cars with a relative. Other performers were more virulent. Ira Louvin called Presley a "white nigger" and criticized him for what was, in effect, musical miscegenation. (Up to that point, country music was strangely free of racism, for all of its connections to Southern culture in the age of Jim Crow. In a booklet he wrote on songwriting, Hank Williams specifically said that a good song would never show prejudice against any race or group of people. Country music was welcoming to one of its great singers, the African-American Charlie Pride. But racial issues often stirred under the surface of the country music subculture.)

Ironically, Elvis maintained his country roots in one major area: his love of gospel music. In fact, Elvis hired a country gospel quartet, the Jordanaires, to be his backup group on most of his early hits. He also recorded some stellar gospel albums.

In those early days of rock and roll, the line between rock and country was not always easy to draw, and many performers crossed over from one to the other. The Everly Brothers were a country act, but their big success was as a teenage group tapping into the new youth market with tunes such as "Bye-bye Love" and "Wake Up Little Susie"—classics of the golden age of rock that were actually produced by country's Chet Atkins. Roy Orbison started with rockabilly, but his unique voice became classified (for no clear reason) as rock and roll. Sometimes the crossovers were from the other side. Conway Twitty started as a rock act, but eventually moved over to country, where he became one of the top country hit-makers. Waylon Jennings started as a guitarist for Buddy Holly and narrowly missed being in his plane the day it went down. Jerry Lee Lewis, the quintessential early rocker (and brother of TV evangelist Jimmy Swaggart), would find lasting success in country music for decades after rock abandoned him.

As the fifties gave way to the sixties—and as rock and roll became the sign and symbol of the counterculture—the lines hardened and turned into battle lines. The flower children mocked country music, associating it with the old-fashioned, retrograde American culture they were rebelling against. Conversely, country music performers and their fans were generally appalled by the hippies and the campus radicals and the revolutionary rhetoric and the whole rock and roll scene. Country music wrapped itself in the American flag and came to represent the "silent majority" whose values were under attack. As the Vietnam War became increasingly divisive—with working-class boys getting killed while college boys protested and rooted for the Viet Cong (at least that is how it was perceived)—feelings grew hotter.

One of country music's greatest artists, Merle Haggard, emerged during this decade, and he took on the counterculture with both guns blazing. In "The Fightin' Side of Me," he expresses annoyance at "people talking bad about the way they have to live here in this country." They are "harpin' on the wars we fight, gripin' 'bout the way things ought to be." He doesn't mind when they stand up for things they believe in. But "when you're runnin' down our country, hoss, you're walkin' on the fightin' side of me." The song even managed to work in the bumper sticker slogan of the silent majority: "If you don't love it, leave it." And Merle, the ex-con, had a way of communicating a sense of menace, which no doubt sent chills down the spines of longhaired flower children who had seen *Easy Rider*. "Let this song that I'm singin' be a warning."

He followed with one of his biggest hits: "Okie from Muskogee." In this song, Haggard drew a line in the sand between two worlds: one where people smoke marijuana, take trips on LSD, burn their draft cards, stage love-ins, wear beads and sandals, let their "hair grow long and shaggy," and disrespect the college dean. The other one is defined by emphatically *not* doing any of those things; instead, they wave Old Glory, pitch woo, wear boots "for manly footwear," play football, respect the college dean—but also drink white lightnin. Muskogee, Oklahoma, U.S.A., is clearly the world of country music and a good part of its fans—the rural, small-town Southwest (where Haggard's parents lived before they joined the Okie migration to Bakersfield, California). As with many of Haggard's songs, this one is about social class. The very word "Okie" in California is a term of ridicule, as Haggard, the son of migrant workers who lived in a labor camp, well knew. As he sings in his poignant "Hungry Eyes," one of the things that caused his mother to suffer was the way that "another class of people put us somewhere just below." Haggard is defiant: he is *proud* to be an Okie. He doesn't care if the cultural elite calls him square. In light of the trends and changes, the fashions and new ideologies, Muskogee, Oklahoma, was the real counterculture.

The song struck a nerve. A number one record, it was voted Song of the Year in 1969 by the Country Music Association.

Actually, Merle Haggard had better rebel credentials than most of the "hippies down in San Francisco." Few of them had done hard time in San Quentin as Merle had. For all of their Marxist rhetoric, not one of them was a champion for the working class like Merle was. (Listen to, for example, his "Working Man Blues.")

Country music was not immune, however, to the larger cultural forces associated with the sixties. No explicitly religious songs made the country charts in that decade. Okies from Muskogee may have been indignant about the sexual revolution, but in truth sexual promiscuity had long been part of the honky-tonk scene. Country fans might not have been smoking marijuana and taking trips on LSD, but truck drivers listening to country radio were "takin' little white pills," as described in Dave Dudley's "Six Days on the Road" (Earl Green, Carl Montgomery); Johnny Cash was recording "Cocaine Blues," with the immortal line, "I took a shot of cocaine and I shot my woman down"; and many performers were struggling with drug problems of the sort that killed Hank Williams.

Country music was reflecting the wider social trends that were making themselves felt even in the Muskogees of the nation. For example, the sixties may have seen the beginnings of the feminist movement, but the women who performed and listened to country music were already asserting themselves. As early as 1952, Hank Thompson had his biggest hit with "The Wild Side of Life" (Arlie A. Carter, William Warren), in which a long-suffering husband chastises his errant wife who frequents the honky-tonks and hangs around with other men. "I didn't know God made honky tonk angels," he sniffs. "I might have known you'd never make a wife."

Irked by this double standard—from Thompson, a performer who was the honky-tonk maestro par excellence—a woman named Kitty Wells came right back with one of the great answer songs, "It Wasn't God Who Made Honky Tonk Angels" (J. D. Miller). To the very same melody, no less, as Hank Thompson's hit, Kitty lets him have it:

> As I sit here tonight the jukebox playing
> The tune about the WILD SIDE OF LIFE
> As I listen to the words you are saying
> It brings mem'ries when I was a trusting wife.

It is the wife who usually gets cheated on, she continues. God doesn't make honky-tonk angels—men do! "Too many times married men think they're still single." That's what causes "many a good girl to go wrong." "It's a shame that all the blame is on us women," she concludes. "From the start most every heart that's ever broken was because there always was a man to blame."

The song spoke to thousands of women and made Kitty Wells a major country star. She was followed by other strong women. No one could tell someone off in a song like Loretta Lynn: "Don't Come Home A-Drinkin' (with Lovin' on Your Mind)," "You Ain't Woman Enough to Take My Man," "You're the Reason Our Kids Are Ugly" (one of her duets with Conway Twitty). She even chronicled the underlying cause of many changes in the role of women in "The Pill."

These women were asserting themselves, but not in the way the radical feminists were. Both Kitty Wells and Loretta Lynn were devout Christians who—unlike many country performers—married for life and valued highly their roles as wives and mothers. Their critique of the mistreatment of women was arguably coming from a Christian perspective rather than that of the radical women's movement. In many ways, the women of country music were also defying the sixties mentality. Tammy Wynette was undoubtedly one of country music's strong women, but she could sing "Stand by Your Man" with defiant conviction, even while recognizing that "sometimes it's hard to be a woman."

Longhaired Rednecks

A funny thing happened in the seventies. The counterculture discovered country music. And country music flirted with the countercultural.

Part of the cultural scene of the sixties was a revival of folk music. From college coffeehouses to the TV show *Hootenanny*, acts such as Peter, Paul, and Mary and the Kingston Trio were in vogue. In this climate, new artists emerged who would ultimately influence the rock scene as well—Bob Dylan, for instance. Folk singers and their fans included genuine aficionados of American traditional music, who were rediscovering for themselves the heritage of Jimmie Rodgers and the Carter Family. Nashville businessmen had allowed bluegrass music to fall into neglect, but it found a new stage at the folk festivals, as Bill Monroe, the Stanley Brothers, and Flatt and Scruggs became big hits among the college crowd.

In the late 1960s and early 1970s, several rock musicians searching for a new sound latched onto elements of country music. Gram Parsons scoured used-record shops in search of out-of-print Louvin Brothers albums so that he could study their harmonies. He joined the already successful band the Byrds, which had delved so deeply into country music that they brought bluegrass virtuoso Clarence White into the band. In 1968, the Byrds released their album *Sweethearts of the Rodeo,* and the hybrid of country rock was born.

Then in 1969, Bob Dylan—who had already gone from acoustic folk music to electrified rock and had become one of the music world's most creative trendsetters—released *Nashville Skyline,* a pure country album. The haunting steel guitars, forthright lyrics, and traditionalism of country seemed quite a switch for Bob the ostensible protest singer. Dylan had become friends with Johnny Cash, doing duets with him on his TV show. Dylan—who had earlier used some of Nashville's top studio musicians in his album *Blonde on Blonde*—actually recorded *Nashville Skyline* in Nashville, drawing on the local talent and thereby introducing them to the rest of the world.

In the meantime, Parsons formed a group of his own, the Flying Burrito Brothers, developing the fusion of country and rock even further. A country flavor seasoned scores of subsequent rock groups, from Lynyrd Skynyrd to the Eagles.

On the country side, Willie Nelson—a long-established Nashville songwriter and performer (he wrote Patsy Cline's "Crazy")—grew out his crewcut and began sporting long hair tied into pigtails, with a bandana around his head. But he didn't change his voice or his innovative yet pure country songs. With his hit album in 1975, *The Red-Headed Stranger,* he managed to appeal to both country purists and the hip generation.

If the staunch conservative American culture represented by country music was overrun by the new waves of the sixties, this at least offered country music some new possibilities. Cultural alienation is good for artists.

The cynicism bred by the Vietnam War, the Watergate crisis, and the disillusionment following the demise of the optimism of the sixties, was felt on nearly every level of American culture. Working-class boys who had been cannon fodder during the Vietnam War, proudly serving with old-fashioned patriotism, came back defeated and unappreciated by the country they had risked their lives for. Economic conditions were shutting down family farms and wreaking havoc in small-town America, forcing many people to the big city, where they didn't want to be. Crime shot up, and both the victims and the perpetrators tended to be from the lower strata of society—a strata that included a large number of country music fans. And even people in Muskogee, Oklahoma, discovered marijuana. They also began to "let their hair grow long and shaggy."

Thus by 1975, Charlie Daniels could write a song like "Long Haired Country Boy" and keep his impeccable country credentials. "People say I'm no good and crazy as a loon," he sings, "'cause I get stoned in the mornin', get drunk in the afternoon." This is no flower child singing, however. Though humorous, the song seethes with class issues about the rich who go to college and the poor who go to work. The song throws the stereotype of the lazy, no-account white trash sleeping on the porch back in the face of the more genteel critics. As for him, he's in a marijuana fog of resignation, apathy, and defiance. (The last stanza says something about a preacher-man on the radio just asking for money. Ironically, Charlie Daniels later became an outspoken Christian—also a cultural conservative who articulated in "Simple Man" the view that drug dealers should be hung on the highest tree and "swing till the sun goes down.")

Even more anarchic was David Allen Coe, with his "Longhaired Redneck" (with Jimmy Rabbit). He describes going into a dive "where bikers stare at cowboys who are laughin' at the hippies, who are prayin' they'll get out of here alive." But it isn't exactly clear where he fits in. Somebody is laughing at his earrings and long hair, not realizing that he has just gotten out of prison and is about to knock the mocker out of his chair. His external appearance might be that of a hippy, but the fact is, he's a low-class, hard-bitten, violent, good ole boy with a prison record. Underneath his long hair is a red neck. Here again is the familiar class resentment, but this time claiming the territory of country music. Although he might look like a hippy, he definitely is "country." The song goes on to prove it, in that he knows all of the songs about Texas and the complete works of Hank Williams. He also invokes Johnny Cash, Johnny Rodriguez (the Hispanic Texan whose promising career fell apart, bottoming out with a murder charge, later ruled justifiable homicide), and the song's cowriter Jimmy Rabbit. And to top it all off, though he looks like Merle Haggard, he sounds like David Allen Coe. Of course, he *is* David Allen Coe. The song, with its intertextuality (referring to and musically alluding to the history and the conventions of country music), its self-parody (the toughness never sounds particularly serious), and its self-referentiality (singing a song in which he is mistaken for himself) is postmodern before postmodern was cool.

The song also mentions Coe's being an "Outlaw." This refers to a whole movement—of which Coe was a hanger-on—led by Waylon Jennings and Willie Nelson, with sixties refugee and former Rhodes scholar Kris Kristofferson playing a role. They were called Outlaws not so much because of a penchant for law-breaking but because they worked outside of the Nashville establishment. As Willie Nelson very publicly pointed out, you did not have to be in Nashville to make it as a country artist. The Outlaws were, for the most part, Texas musicians. They scorned the commercialism and corporate pressures of the music industry, with its manufactured images and artistic compromises to get airtime. They found that there were more live music joints in Austin than there were in Nashville and that they could make a living and win fans outside of the Nashville scene.

The Outlaws cultivated the image of rough individualism associated with the Wild West. Instead of rhinestone suits, they wore blue jeans and workshirts (with boots and Stetsons, of course). They grew long hair and beards like the old gunfighters and added marijuana smoking to their beer drinking.

The University of Texas provided a huge audience, as college kids who might have been hippies in the previous decade found that they could accomplish the same thing by being, what was somewhat derisively termed, "Cosmic Cowboys." The term came from a song by Michael Martin Murphy, who would later become a serious student and popularizer of traditional cowboy music. Some of these countrified hippies proved to be talented performers, such as Jimmie Dale Gilmore. Some veterans of country rock crossed all the way over into hard-core country, such as Emmylou Harris. The stimulating musical climate of Texas in the 1970s produced a whole slew of original new artists, such as Joe Ely and Townes Van Zandt.

Perhaps paradoxically, this Texas brand of country music tended to be more traditional than what Nashville music had become. While the big Nashville studios were adding lush strings and overblown orchestral arrangements to George Jones vocals, the Texas artists were paring down and going back to the fiddle and steel guitar. The Outlaw sound brought back and reemphasized the old conventions and motifs, from honky-tonk revelry to bleak confessions, that had become somewhat obscured behind Nashville's recent slicker sounds. The Texas scene, despite—or perhaps because of—its countercultural fellow travelers, would pave the way for the New Traditionalism of the 1980s.

Back to the Country

The Ronald Reagan decade was a good time for country music. The old silent majority—the patriots, the anticommunists, the cultural conservatives—turned out to have been right after all, or so it seemed. The 1980s actually marked a neoconservatism, which was by no means the same as the old conservatism, being more permissive, stressing freedom more than control, and embracing change. If the Reagan administration marked a "springtime for America"—an era of new optimism and new confidence in American values, after the trauma and self-doubt of the Vietnam years—it was also a springtime (however short-lived) for country music.

The decade began with a huge breakthrough in popularity for country music. By this time, rock and roll was in decline, having degenerated into the theatrics and feather boas of glam rock and the synthetic rhythms of disco. John Travolta had popularized the latter in *Staying Alive* during the seventies, but in 1980 when he appeared in a new dance movie, *Urban Cowboy*, many trendsetters were ready for a change. The movie was based on a New Journalism piece in *Esquire Magazine* that chronicled the sad lives of displaced rural Texans who now had to work in the big-city oil refineries, finding escape in Mickey Gilley's dance hall, with its faux-western poseurs and its mechanical bull. Perhaps missing the elegiac meaning, hundreds of former discos put in mechanical bulls and started giving line-dance lessons, and thousands of neophyte Urban Cowboys bought hats and boots and started buying country music.

Like all fads, this one didn't last long. The Urban Cowboys, like the succession of Drugstore Cowboys, Rhinestone Cowboys, and Cosmic Cowboys, may have been poseurs, but they showed that country music was stepping outside of its old rural, Southern, working-class base and finding brand-new followers. Thus, Barbara Mandrell could make the proud claim in her song in the early eighties that "I Was Country When Country Wasn't Cool" (Kye Fleming, Dennis W. Morgan). Country had never been cool before.

In the eighties, it appeared that the country music world had survived the turmoil of its previous problems, both internal and external. Country music had survived the rock and roll onslaught. It had also survived the arguably misguided solution to its declining popularity—the Nashville sound, with its grandiose string orchestras and pop stylings.

Moreover, the former Outlaws had been accepted into the fold. Willie Nelson led the charts for the entire decade. More important than Nelson's Outlaw image was the fact that he had become a success largely on his own terms, not within Nashville's accepted methodology. This encouraged other artists—and Nashville itself—to change.

While country music seemed comfortable with itself as the decade began, it was clear that there were many disaffected or disenfranchised country music lovers searching for a sound different from the clichés of country radio. Outlaw music alone wouldn't do, though. People were no longer in a rebellious mood. They yearned for something fresh yet traditional, the values of the past expressed in a positive, contemporary way.

When George Strait's first single, "Unwound," hit the radio waves in the spring of 1981, it was like the fresh scent of a Texas field of bluebonnets. Here was the sound. Here was the man. Popular with audiences and performers, Strait ushered in the New Traditionalist movement.

Although not known as a rebel, in the way of the Outlaws before him or many of the New Traditionalists to follow, Strait knew exactly what he was after, in terms of both music and image. First of all, he was a real cowboy—not an Urban, Rhinestone, or Cosmic Cowboy—a rodeo steer-roper who lived on a ranch in Texas. Clean-cut, with what Charlie Louvin called a "real boy's haircut," Strait eschewed both the rhinestone Nudie suits of Nashville (named after the designer, a Mr. Nudie) and the scruffy proletariat garb of the longhaired Outlaws. He wore neat Wranglers, a western shirt, and—above all—his cowboy hat. When he was signed by MCA, studio executives wanted him to get rid of his hat, feeling it was an antiquated look—perhaps too cowboy or too country for them to handle and not in keeping with the new status of country being cool. But Strait refused to give up his hat. He set the precedent for scores of so-called hat acts in the next two decades. More important than the look and the image, however, was the immediate impact his music had on other performers who had thought real country music was dead.

Texas music scholar Tony Davidson recalls, "By the early 1980s I had seen most of the big names, but the first time I saw George Strait in Bryan, Texas, I couldn't believe the reaction he was getting. Women going absolutely nuts by the stage, throwing themselves at him, and the men tolerating it all because the music was so . . . good. That was new; I'd never seen anything like it."[3]

Strait breathed new life into the old heartbreak songs, but he also brought back the upbeat mood and the musical style of western swing. Not a songwriter himself, Strait had a genius for finding and interpreting beautiful melodies.

His influence and precedent-setting success plowed the way for other performers, as Nashville studios suddenly became open to performers for whom "new" and "traditional" were not a contradiction in terms. Dwight Yoakam says that he had just decided to stop performing, convinced that there was no market for his brand of honky-tonk music. Then he heard George Strait's "Unwound" getting radio play and decided to give it one more try. Yoakam's album *Guitars, Cadillacs, Etc., Etc.* in 1986 resurrected California country—the Bakersfield sound. Yoakam rescued Buck Owens from years of *Hee Haw* reruns, coaxing him out of retirement and paying tribute—both musically and personally—to the man who introduced the hot electric guitar leads of his bandmember Don Rich into country music.

Another talented performer who walked through the door that George Strait had opened (now that record executives knew this kind of music could sell), was Randy Travis, whose expressive voice sounds as if it were on loan from Lefty Frizzell. Travis himself has credited timing for his success. He acknowledges the importance of hard work and talent, but he is well aware that he came along at the right time. This seems likely, considering that Travis had released his first single in 1979 and saw it flop. But by 1985, his singles such as "On the Other Hand" and "Forever and Ever, Amen," were heard everywhere—songs that were as traditional in their values as they were in their sound.

The momentum of the New Traditionalists began to stall in the latter part of the decade, however. Travis, Strait, and Yoakam were still successful on the charts, but apparently they were not influencing others to the pure sound they embraced. At least no other traditional-sounding acts were being signed by the major labels and getting airplay. Of the three, only George Strait consistently produced hits, with Dwight and Randy seeing most of the 1990s off the radio.

In the meantime, country music found its biggest star ever, a man who sold more records than Elvis and brought more new listeners to country music than anyone else in its history: Garth Brooks. Scores of performers and studios tried to emulate his style, his look, and his capacity to break into the pop market. Other megastars emerged, many of whom paid their dues in the previous decades: Reba McIntire, Brooks and Dunn, Vince Gill (Oklahomans all, as was Garth—if the previous two decades were dominated by Texans, the 1990s were dominated by Okies). The so-called class of 1989 included not only Garth but also two very different singers—Alan Jackson and Clint Black. They all made their debuts the same year and would graduate into superstardom. And yet, as we shall see, in the last decade of the century, country music began to be a victim of its own success.

But through the cultural changes reflected in country music, through all of the decades since the Bristol Sessions, from the Carter Family to Garth Brooks, certain themes and motifs, emotions and obsessions, kept manifesting themselves. Country music persisted in dealing with issues of despair and faith, sin and grace, the destruction of families and the building of families. The beliefs, failings, and commitments of the old traditions have not changed all that much.

The Christian Tradition in Country Music

BETWEEN THE DEVIL AND ME

One style of country music, more than any other, has self-consciously kept alive the old country traditions—both musically and ideologically. Bluegrass, a relatively new creation, was founded by Bill Monroe. Monroe took the strains of mountain music, established a fixed mode of acoustic instrumentation (fiddle, mandolin, guitar, bass, and banjo), all set at breakneck speed in an improvisational style that owes more to jazz than the one-melody unison approach of the old string bands. But Monroe loved what he called "the ancient tones," and the art form he founded preserves both the old tunes and the old ideas. In bluegrass, it is evident how the sacred and the secular not only exist side by side musically, but how they interpenetrate each other, constituting a total worldview in which Christian faith is a part of everyday life in all of its joys, sorrows, and travails.

Ralph Stanley, one of the great pioneers of bluegrass, says, "Of the 170 albums I've played on, about 40 percent are gospel."[1] A similar mixture of sacred and secular numbers can be found on nearly every bluegrass album by nearly every performer. Contemporary bluegrass virtuoso—and country music crossover— Alison Krauss told a reporter, "I'm trying to remember a [bluegrass] band that doesn't play gospel. I just can't think of any."[2] Even the popularizing 1972 bluegrass anthology *Will the Circle Be Unbroken*, which featured the folk-rock Nitty Gritty Dirt Band playing with legends such as Maybelle Carter and Earl Scruggs, has a good half-dozen religious songs. On the 1993 anthology album from Rounder Records, *Blue Ribbon Bluegrass*, "River of Jordan" and "When God Dips His Love in My Heart" take their place next to "Girl at the Roadside Inn" and "Lonesome River." The album also features songs like "Lost and I'll Never Find the Way" and "Here Today and Gone Tomorrow," where the sacred and the secular cannot be separated from each other.

Though not in such pure strains as in bluegrass, the spiritual and the earthy continue to coexist in mainstream country music as well. As country music has become part of the popular music industry, reaching a larger and more diverse mass audience, some of the Christianity has lost its edge or has become nearly unrecognizable. Nevertheless, the place of Christianity in American culture, particularly in American rural and working-class cultures, runs deep. Even in contemporary country music the Christian tradition continues to leave its mark.

The whole array of songs about breakups and alcoholism, guilt and remorse (which will be discussed in chapters 7 and 8) can be seen in terms of the old revival testimonies, exemplifying the sinner's confession. Today, however, the grace that was the substance of the gospel songs—the forgiveness of sin through Christ—is often conspicuously absent.

Exhortations also continue to be a common theme in country music. Straightforward advice about how the listener ought to live is a staple of the genre, from the Carter Family's "Keep on the Sunny Side" to the Louvin Brothers' "Love Thy Neighbor As Thyself" to Clint Black's "Wherever You Go (There You Are)" (with Hayden Nicholas). Even modern country superstar Garth Brooks is fond of exhorting his legions of listeners as to how they should live their lives. These exhortations include the faintly Christian "The River" (with Victoria Shaw) ("with the good Lord as my captain" he can sail his vessel through the rough waters); the call for bold action in "Standing Outside the Fire" (with Jenny Yates) ("Life is not tried, it is merely survived/If you're standing outside the fire"); and the rather relativistic "Do What You Gotta Do" (Pat Flynn).

Country music historian Ronnie Pugh classifies several motifs of the old country gospel songs, a large number of which continue to appear in the bluegrass repertoire. They include the Bible, religious experience, personal morality, eternity, the country church, and life as a pilgrimage.[3] Many of these motifs still manifest themselves in country music also—sometimes intact and sometimes in altered or oddly displaced variations.

The Bible

The Bible is a motif that looms large in country gospel, befitting the centrality of the Word of God in Southern Protestant churches. Examples include old songs such as "I'm Using My Bible for a Roadmap," the Blue Sky Boys' "B-I-B-L-E," and the Bailes Brothers' "Dust on the Bible," recorded by Kitty Wells and others. And, of course, the previously discussed "Little Log Cabin by the Sea" by the Carter Family, with its "precious, precious Bible."

The Bible remains a potent image in contemporary country music. Willie Nelson wrote a moving song called "Family Bible" (before he sold the songwriting rights). George Jones recorded a tune called "Mama's Family Bible" (L. Kingston), and more recently, Randy Travis recorded "The Family Bible and the Farmer's Almanac" (Lee Thomas Miller, Bob Regan). In Travis' hit "The Box" (with Buck Moore), a family goes through a collection of memorabilia that had been treasured by the father who recently died, revealing depths of feeling and character they had never known, because of his strong, taciturn, rocklike exterior. Among his possessions in the box was "the faded Bible he had got when he was baptized," leading to the conclusion, "I guess nobody understood him but the Lord."

In Mark Chesnutt's "Thank God for Believers" (Mark Alan Springer, Roger Springer, Tim Johnson) an alcoholic husband, off the wagon again, staggers home to his hurt, worried, but constant wife, who has been praying for him, crying, and seeking strength in the Scriptures. He sees "the hurt in her eyes" and "the Bible on the table where she prayed." The Bible is a poignant sign of the wife's piety and faith—not only in God but in her backsliding husband as well. The "believers" of the song title refers to the way his wife unaccountably believes in him, which inspires him to battle his drinking problem. The love and forgiveness of the wife is a secular counterpart to the grace of God, who likewise offers sinners forgiveness that can change them from the inside. Although the song is about human love, the title, "Thank God for Believers," and the image of the Bible places this family drama in the context of evangelical theology.

Religious Experience

Religious experience—that is, conversion, prayer, and praise—is another, rather obvious, motif of country gospel cited by Pugh. Examples of this motif include nearly all of the old revival songs as well as the works of country gospel groups such as the Bailes Brothers ("One Way Ticket to the Sky," "You Can't Go Half Way [and Get In]"). The pious effusions of songwriters such as Odell McLeod ("From the Manger to the Cross") and Red Foley ("Steal Away," "Just a Closer Walk with Thee") became staples of the Grand Ole Opry.

Perhaps the greatest country artist in both singing and writing songs explicitly about religious experience was Hank Williams, his most famous example being "I Saw the Light." (He deserves a chapter unto himself, chapter 9.)

More recently, Johnny Cash has been singing songs of conversion, such as "Unchained" (Jude Johnstone). The singer recounts how he has been ungrateful, unwise, and restless. On his knees, he confesses his weakness and vanity and asks God to "take this weight from me/Let my spirit be unchained."

Cash's album of the same title mingles the regular array of crime songs and traveling songs with numerous songs of religious experience. These include the wrenching and desperate "Spiritual" (Josh Haden):

> Jesus, I don't wanna die alone;
> Jesus, oh Jesus, I don't wanna die alone.
> My love wasn't true
> Now all I have is you.
> Jesus, oh Jesus, I don't wanna die alone.
> Jesus, if you hear my last breath,
> Don't leave me here,
> Left to die a lonely death.
> I know I have sinned,
> But Lord I'm suffering.

The album also includes songs of spiritual peace ("Memories Are Made of This" [Frank Miller, Richard Dehr, Terry Gilkyson]) and ecstasy (Cash's own "Meet Me in Heaven").

Praise is a subcategory of religious experience, often appearing in contemporary country music in the context of a song celebrating ordinary life. Songs that thank the good Lord for love or marriage or family are fairly common. These range from Tennessee Ernie Ford's classic rendition of "Count Your Many Blessings" (John Oatman Jr., Edwin O. Excell) to Alison Krauss' lovely "In the Palm of Your Hand" (Ron Block), with its clear christological assurance. "If I trust the one who died for me,/Who shed His blood to set me free," she sings, she can have confidence that for her physical needs His grace will provide.

A particularly charming example of praise is Tracy Byrd's hit "The Keeper of the Stars" (Dickey Lee, Danny Bear Mayo, Karen Ruth Staley). It couldn't have been an accident finding the woman he married, he reflects. It was God's providence. • **75**

He just can't believe she is in his life. "I tip my hat to the keeper of the stars/He sure knew what he was doin'" when He joined them together. The singer is so overwhelmed with love for his wife and awe at how their lives have come together that he is filled with praise for God, expressed in the cowboy gesture of "tipping his hat" to the Lord.

The religious experience of prayer is also common in country music, generally in the context of anguish and trouble. An example notable for its direct Christian and biblical imagery—and for being a hit record by the teen heartthrob Bryan White—is "One Small Miracle" (Bill Anderson, Steve Wariner). In this song, a man desperately asks Jesus to perform a miracle to keep his wife from leaving him:

> She's standing at the front door
> With her suitcase in her hand
> I'm starin' down the hallway
> Frozen where I stand.
>
> She says she doesn't love me anymore
> Oh, Lord, what can I do
> It's gonna take a miracle to make her stay
> That's why I'm askin' You.
>
> I know I haven't been a Saint
> And asking You for anything takes nerve
> 'Cause You've already blessed me
> With so much more in life than I deserve.
>
> But if You can make a blind man see
> And change the water into wine
> Surely You can keep her from
> Tearin' out this old heart of mine.

In a more upbeat mood, another contemporary artist, Pam Tillis, sings about praying to meet the right man in "I Said a Prayer" (Leslie Satcher), a prayer, she sings exuberantly, that was answered.

And then there is Garth Brooks and "Unanswered Prayers." Brooks wrote the song, he says, based on an incident that actually occurred. The song tells of a man and his wife who attend a high school football game while visiting his hometown. Here, he runs into an old girlfriend whom he had such a crush on in high school that he had prayed for God to bring them together. He introduces her to his wife, and they chat awkwardly, without much to say. His old girlfriend isn't quite the angel he had remembered; time has changed them both. As she walks away, he turns and looks at his wife and is filled with gratitude that God did not grant his adolescent prayer. God's plan is better than our own. Since "the Lord knows what He's doin' after all," the singer reflects that "some of God's greatest gifts are unanswered prayers." The song, from his first album, is one of Brooks' most endearing and combines both prayer and praise.

Although religious experience is an acceptable subject for country music, some country songs today retain religious language and imagery but use it in a very different way. The biblical language is there, but it is displaced away from God, referring instead to human and even sexual love. This is not a totally new thing—seventeenth-century English poet John Donne did something similar, using erotic imagery in his religious poems to God, and religious imagery in his love poems. But the country way of transposing such imagery falls somewhat short of the metaphysical.

Thus, in "Amen Kind of Love" (Trey Bruce, Wayne Tester), Daryle Singletary uses evangelical imagery to describe the effect of a new girlfriend. For the first time he sees the light (alluding to Hank Williams' "I Saw the Light"). Now the Spirit moves him to testify about a love that brings him to his knees. The love affair is described with images from a Pentecostal revival—the Holy Spirit, testifying, getting slain in the Spirit, and shouting "Amen!" The song goes on to allude to traditional hymns and gospel songs: "Safe in your faithful arms I am leaning" ("Leaning on the Everlasting Arms") and "Once I was lost but now I am found for ever more" ("Amazing Grace"). • **77**

The profanation is taken even farther in "Brand New Man" written and performed by Brooks and Dunn. "I saw the light," the singer testifies. Not only that, "I've been baptized." Not by water and the Word, not even by the Holy Spirit's fire as Pentecostalists like to think of it. Rather, he was baptized "by the fire in your touch/and the flame in your eyes." This experience makes him "born to love again," transforming him into a "brand new man." Here, in the very first line, Hank Williams' classic song is directly appropriated, wrenched away from God, and applied to the way a woman makes him feel. The song then proceeds to do the same thing with baptism, the fire of the Holy Spirit, and the phrase "born again." As the song continues, it is evident that these are not mere figures of speech; rather, it is, in fact, a conversion song. But it is not conversion through Christ; it is conversion through the love of a good woman. He "used to have a wild side" and would "burn those beer joints down." But now he is walking the line. "You turned my life around." The secularization of the gospel tradition is here complete. The religious imagery, however, is retained and remains potent; only its object has been changed.

To his credit, George Strait pulls off the reverse, moving from human love to divine love. In "Love without End, Amen" (Aaron Barker), he sings about getting in trouble for fighting and being afraid to face his father. "Let me tell you a secret about a father's love," he is told. "Daddies don't just love their children every now and then/It's a love without end, Amen." Then, in the familiar country narrative pattern, the next stanza has the singer with his own son. "That stubborn boy was just like my father's son." In response to his own son now getting into trouble, the message about the unconditional quality of a father's love is passed on to the next generation. In the final stanza, the singer dreams he has died and is standing outside the pearly gates. "If they know half the things I've done, they'll never let me in." But then he hears those same words from his heavenly Father, who has "a love without end, Amen." The religious, even liturgical, language of the chorus is returned to its original theological context. Salvation is by grace, not works. The divine truth is indeed manifested in human and family relationships, which point to a reality beyond themselves. Yes, the song is sentimental, and yes, its theology leaves out the role of the "father's son," namely, Christ. But Strait pulls off this little emblem of grace amazingly well.

Personal Morality

Personal morality, construed in terms of private charity and concern for one's neighbor, is another theme of country gospel cited by Ronnie Pugh. Pugh emphasizes that in the old country gospel songs, the way to a better society is through personal action, not through any kind of political activism or collectivist schemes.

To the consternation of liberal activists and Marxist academics, America's working class—particularly in the South—tends to be conservative. To be sure, as the group Alabama sings in "Song of the South," the region has been dominated by the "Southern Democrat," who, stung by the Depression, believes that "Mr. Roosevelt is gonna save us all" through public works programs such as the TVA. And yet, though poor whites, farmers, and blue-collar workers might be expected to have financial interests that would push them in the direction of political radicalism—as in the case of the Socialist parties of Europe—they have a cultural conservatism that confounds "progressive" politicians.

A major reason for Southern conservatism may be the theology and the history of the Southern church. As Pugh points out, the old gospel songs have nothing to do with the "social gospel" that had taken hold in mainline Northern denominations as early as the nineteenth century, accelerating into the twentieth. According to the social gospel, which attempts to accommodate the modernist claims of progress and its rejection of the supernatural in favor of the scientific, the old personal gospel of individual salvation is outmoded. The church needs instead to be involved in saving society. The great social reform movements of the nineteenth century—Abolition, Prohibition, Women's

Suffrage—as well as programs to ban child labor, clean up the slums, and otherwise address issues of economic justice in an industrial economy, were in large measure fueled by Christians trying to carry out the social gospel.

For conservative churches, including the vast number of those in the South, the social gospel was heresy, a blatant rejection of the Word of God. Individual salvation is at the essence of Christianity, which is about saving the souls of sinners for eternal life. To replace the saving gospel of Christ with do-good schemes that promise a utopia on earth through political action is a satanic distortion. That the modernist theologians sided with the evolutionists in the aftermath of the Scopes Trial in Tennessee intensified the issue. Much later, the Southern churches became politically active, motivated by issues such as legalized abortion, but the battles fought by the so-called Christian Right were moral and cultural rather than economic.

It might be said that theological liberals tend to be tolerant of personal moral failings, pushing their moral concerns out to the periphery of vast social causes. Voting responsibly and holding the correct positions on global peace and the environment are of greater moral significance than, for example, their own sexual behavior. Conservative Christians, on the other hand, focus on the moral responsibility of the individual, as expressed tangibly in his or her own actions and relationships with others. The big social issues are too distant, too far removed, to have much moral significance. At least this is the stance in country gospel and, for the most part, in country music.

Early songs about concern for one's neighbor include "Love Thy Neighbor As Thyself," "The Gospel Way," "The Sons and Daughters of God," "Pray for Me," and "That's All That He's Asking of Me"—from the Louvin Brothers' repertoire alone. The emphasis in all of these songs is helping your neighbor down the road, not any vast social reform.

Even in contemporary country music, songs of social responsibility tend to be songs of individuals helping individuals. These range from George Jones' tearjerker about the homeless ("Wild Irish Rose") to Shania Twain's plea for suffering children ("God Bless the Child," whose Christian warrant is further established by the refrain of "Hallelujah").

A hit by Mark Wills, "Don't Laugh at Me," enjoins listeners not to make fun of geeks, children who are chosen last, fat people, crippled beggars, or the down-and-out who hold up cardboard signs asking for work. The basis for this request for benevolence is theological: everyone is equal before God, and everyone is an immortal soul designed for eternal life, when "we'll all have perfect wings."

Then there is Martina McBride's odd country rap, "Love's the Only House" (Tom Douglas, Buzz Cason), which surveys the pain in the world, from the grocery store line to the sights from a car window. After rehearsing a variety of encounters, the song is resolved back in the grocery store when a single mother doesn't have enough money to cover the cost of milk for her baby. The singer pays for the carton of milk and invites her home. The refrain is the quasi-theological "Love's the only house big enough for all the pain in the world," and the answer is to "come down and get my hands dirty and together we'll make a stand." Again, the answer is not vast social reform but individuals helping individuals in concrete ways.

Collin Raye had two big hits with more complex moral exhortations. In "I Think About You" (Don Schlitz, Steve Seskin), the singer surveys the way women are used and abused, thinking all along of his eight-year-old daughter. Sex objects suddenly become humanized. When a movie actress "plays Lolita in some old man's dreams," he thinks about his daughter. When he sees men leering at a pretty woman, "like she's some kind of treat," he thinks about her. He becomes sensitive to all mistreatment of women. When he hears about a woman who has been "abandoned or abused/It doesn't matter who she is/I think about you." This moral meditation amounts to an application of the Golden Rule: he would not like his own daughter treated in these ways. It also brings the treatment of women, in a way characteristic of many country songs, into the realm of family values. He realizes "That every woman used to be/Somebody's little girl." Every woman used to be a little girl like his eight-year-old, with a father who probably felt about her the way he feels about his daughter. The protectiveness he feels for his daughter is projected onto all women.

In Raye's other exhortation, "What If Jesus Comes Back Like That?" (Pat Bunch, Doug Johnson), social and moral issues are portrayed in an explicitly Christocentric way. The singer gives a vivid description of a hobo—"low-down no-account white trash"—and a crack baby, "born with a habit of drug abuse/she couldn't help what her mama used." After each description, he raises the shocking question: What if this despised and rejected human being turns out to be Jesus?

> What if Jesus comes back like that,
> Two months early and hooked on crack?
> Will we let him in or turn our backs?
> What if Jesus comes back like that?
> Oh what if Jesus comes back like that?

After all, no one would let Jesus in the first time, when "he came to town on a cold dark night . . . a manger for his bed." This is not just a matter of benevolence, as one might find with a more liberal theology; judgment is at stake. As the New Testament warns, the way we receive others may reflect the way Jesus receives us:

> What if Jesus comes back like that?
> Will he cry when he sees where our hearts are at?
> Will he let us in or turn his back?

Raye invokes Christ's sorrow, but also His judgment. What if He turns His back on us? What if He doesn't let *us* in? The song may be confused in its eschatology, but its biblical text is Matthew 25:40: "Inasmuch as ye have done it unto one of the least of these my brethren, ye have done it unto me." The song is a remarkable meditation on how Christ is hidden in weakness, suffering, and those the world despises—what Luther explored as "the theology of the cross." In fact, the song applies the lesson of the cross—His and ours, and the relationship between them—in so many words:

Nobody said life is fair
We've all got a cross to bear
When it gets a little hard to care
Just think of Him hanging there.

Eternal Punishment and Eternal Life

Another common motif in early country gospel is eternity—what happens after death. Actually, Pugh focuses on eternal punishment, the image of the hellfire of God's judgment that awaits those who reject salvation. We extend this category somewhat to include the evocations of heaven that await the saved. Images of heaven and hell were staples of early gospel, and both continue—sometimes in oddly distorted forms—in country music today.

The old-time country churches were famous for their hell-fire-and-brimstone preaching, and this imagery is indeed reflected in many gospel songs. But these were gospel songs, so the lurid spectacle of damnation was nearly always employed for the purpose of urging sinners to escape such a fate by embracing the free salvation offered by Christ.

Thus we have songs such as "Satan Is Real" and "Satan's Jeweled Crown" by the Louvin Brothers. Then there are songs that vividly describe the wrath of God in terms drawn from everyday life, such as Bill Monroe's "He Will Set Your Fields on Fire" (C. M. Ballew, L. L. Brackett). Sometimes such lyrics go beyond mere scary imagery to describe the misery of a lost soul in earthly life as well, the inner spiritual state that is fixed forever apart from grace, as in "The Lost Highway" (Leon Payne) and "The Devil Train" (Hank Williams). Many of these songs of judgment are cast in apocalyptic terms, fitting with the premillennial anticipations of Christ's return that preoccupied many Southern churches.

Again, these songs were not designed to scare the listener. They were evangelistic. The terror that awaits those who have broken God's law is presented as a reason to embrace the free gift of salvation. For example, in the Bailes Brothers' song "The Pale Horse and His Rider" (recorded by Hank Williams), the vividly eerie figures from the Book of Revelation (6:8), embodiments of death and hell, are merely part of a plea for the sinner to turn to Christ: "If you're not saved; you'll be lost in the night/When the Pale Horse and his rider goes by."

In "Wait a Little Longer Please Jesus" (Chester Smith, Hazel Houser)—an old tune later recorded by Merle Haggard—the singer actually asks Jesus to wait a while before coming back so that there will be more time to evangelize the lost, including (poignant touch) the members of his own family who do not know Christ: "Just a little longer, please Jesus,/A few more days to get our loved ones in."

Contrary to what one might expect, these evangelistic songs are not self-righteous or moralistic, nor are they directed at specific transgressors. Everyone stands under God's judgment, apart from Christ. Often a "friend" or "poor soul" is addressed, and the tone, though harrowing, is one of earnest caring.

But even images of the apocalypse can be secularized. In "The Great Atomic Power," the Louvin Brothers, writing in the shadow of the Cold War, conflate the coming of Christ with the atomic bomb. Meeting the Savior in the air is described in terms of vaporized bodies. The Louvins cut both ways with their brand of gospel, simultaneously dramatizing God's wrath by comparing heavenly power to an atomic weapon, and yet portraying Christ as someone you'll be glad to meet "in the clouds."

Another kind of infernal imagery is that of the devil roaming the earth, leading people into temptation. Sometimes he is just a colorful opponent, as in Charlie Daniels' "The Devil Went Down to Georgia," about a fiddle contest between the devil and a Georgia farmboy. Contests with the devil are an old folk motif. A cowboy song called "Tying Knots in the Devil's Tale" has two cowhands bulldogging the devil, like any other horned animal.

The devil as tempter appears in many songs, including songs that are quite contemporary. In "From Hillbilly Heaven, to Honky Tonk Hell" (Michael Huffman, Woody Mullis, Mike Geiger), singers George Jones and Tracie Lawrence describe how a man lost his paradise—his country girl bride, living in a double-wide trailer out in the country. This country music Eden is lost when he falls because of the allure of the city. At the honky-tonk, he finds temptation and takes the forbidden fruit of another woman. He goes "from a warm home fire burning/To a cold, cheap motel." His wife, described as an "angel," is left hurt and crying, while the unfaithful husband loses his marriage and home—and will presumably be bewailing his lonesomeness and his wrecked life, along with the other characters in honky-tonk songs.

The devil also figures in songs about alcoholism, such as Kenny Chesney's plaintive "That's Why I'm Here" (Shaye Smith, Mark Alan Springer), which combines descriptions of Alcoholics Anonymous meetings and twelve-step talk with recognition of the devil, who had a hand in his fall and his loss.

In Alan Jackson's hit, "Between the Devil and Me" (Harley Allen, Carson Chamberlain), the only thing between the singer and the fires of hell is the love of a good woman. The world is tempting. There is a right road and a wrong road. His own flesh is weak. "The gates of hell swing open wide, invitin' me to step inside." The devil himself is beckoning. But through the flames and smoke of hell, he sees the one he loves. "She's all I see between the devil and me."

This is the time-honored motif, particularly common in American literature, of the domesticating woman who saves the man from his worst impulses. But in this song, it is not Jesus who saves the man from the world, the flesh, and the devil; it is the man's wife. The biblical imagery of temptation, damnation, and hell is very alive and has lost none of its potency. But to a large degree it has become secularized.

As with songs of religious experience, songs of heaven and hell today often refer not to eternal life but to human love.

Willie Nelson puts it bluntly in "Heaven or Hell" (a song performed by Waylon Jennings). Heaven is not a place paved with gold, and hell is not a place of fire. "Heaven is lying in my sweet baby's arms/Hell is when my baby's not there." In fact, in song after song, heaven has become a metaphor for sexual pleasure.

Thus we have Mark Wills' scoring a hit with "Jacob's Ladder" (Tony Martin, Cal and Brenda Sweat) about a poor boy named Jacob who uses a ladder to climb up to his girlfriend's room. "Heaven was waitin' at the top of Jacob's ladder." Jacob's girlfriend is named Rachel—the writers obviously knew their Bible, but the biblical allusions are gutted of their content and twisted into a very different kind of message.

One of the more blasphemous songs in country music may be "Heaven's Just a Sin Away" (Jerry Gillespie), sung by the Kendalls. A sweet, little-girl voice sings about giving in to sexual temptation. "Heaven's just a sin away, oh, oh, just a sin away/I can't wait another day I think I'm givin' in." She knows it's wrong, but she longs to be with him tonight. She knows the devil is tempting her, but—the song is punctuated throughout by panting oh, ohs—she is giving in. Such is the allure of sensual "heaven." The song, sung with nearly pornographic eagerness, is full of Bible talk, but it is horribly twisted: The way to "heaven" is to sin. A number one hit in 1977, the song is made even creepier by the fact that the Kendalls are a father-daughter duet. What father would even let his daughter sing a song like this?

Of course, the orthodox heaven is also a recurrent theme in country music. Most often heaven is imagined not just in terms of pearly gates and streets of gold but as the place of reunion with family and loved ones after death. This is evident from the Carter Family's "Will the Circle Be Unbroken" to, more recently, Johnny Cash's composition "Meet Me in Heaven." The singer recalls their life together, the troubles, pain, love, and laughter that they shared. We can't be sure what it is going to be like after death. But they will know each other in heaven. The song goes on to describe a deep spiritual intimacy. "We've seen the secret things revealed by God." And it ends by squarely facing death and eternity: "Will you meet me in Heaven someday?" This song is apparently addressed to Johnny's wife, June Carter, making it something of a reprise of her family's most famous song about the family circle being unbroken "bye and bye."

The prospect of heaven has largely driven out the prospect of hell in today's country music. The earlier music was often full of brimstone, but just as even many evangelical churches have since toned down threats of eternal damnation—or at least stopped talking so much about it—today's country music leans toward a cheerful universalism. Even criminals about to be hung think they are headed for heaven, as in Porter Waggoner's "The Green, Green Grass of Home" (Curly Putman) or Merle Haggard's "Sing Me Back Home." Often heaven becomes embarrassingly sentimentalized, as in Steve Wariner's "Holes in the Floor of Heaven," which he both wrote and performed. It is about a little boy whose grandma dies, whereupon his mother tells him that heaven has holes in its floor. This means his grandma can look down through the holes in the floor and see what is happening to him. Furthermore, when it rains, those are her tears leaking through those same holes. In the course of the song, the boy grows up and gets married, but then the wife dies, again calling to mind heaven's perforated flooring. And as if that were not enough, the final stanza includes the other surefire tearjerking scenario of the same man giving away his daughter in marriage. It is raining, so the daughter consoles her dad by pointing out how mama is looking down and crying through those holes. Not only was this a monster hit for Steve Wariner, it was named 1998 Song of the Year by the Country Music Association. The success of this song, as late as 1998, demonstrates the continued appeal of eternal life songs, even as it shows how they have slipped in biblical seriousness. (The Bailes Brothers or the Louvin Brothers or Hank Williams might point out that heaven's floor is paved with gold and is thus presumably leakproof.)

And yet, even modern, mainline country music still recognizes the real thing. Vince Gill had a hit in 1994 with "Go Rest

High on That Mountain," a moving tribute he wrote on the death of his brother, who had been mentally handicapped. The song treats this wrenching topic with honest emotion, without a shred of sentimentality. He recognizes that his brother's life was troubled and filled with pain. But as the family gathers around his brother's grave the emotions are tempered with the hope and the joy of his eternal life. His work is done. He can go into his rest. He can "Go to heaven a-shoutin'/Love for the Father and the Son." Heaven, like the gospel, offers rest from our work. It is also a place of singing. The brother goes to his heavenly rest shouting with love for God the Father and His Son, the Savior Jesus Christ. The song is not only an orthodox depiction of the Christian heaven, it is framed in trinitarian terms.

6

The Christian Tradition in Country Music

OLD RUINED CHURCHES

The figure of the church is another motif of early country gospel. As Ronnie Pugh points out, the church specifically has to be an *old* church, and it has to be a *rural* church.

The importance of this distinction is again due to the schism between fundamentalists and modernists. There was truly a difference between "That Old Time Religion" and the attenuated this-worldliness of mainline modernist churches, which minimized the Bible in favor of modern thought and substituted the social gospel of political activism for personal salvation through Christ. Small, poor, rural churches were more likely to hew to the old-time religion than the urban churches of the upper crust.

Churches derided as "fundamentalist" had a theological chip on their shoulders. Note the defiance in Roy Acuff's trademark song, "The Great Speckled Bird" (Guy Smith), a rather labored midrash of Jeremiah 12:9: "Mine heritage is unto me as a speckled bird." The song concludes that the bird symbolizes the true church. Not that there aren't other churches, but they oppose the speckled bird. They envy the true church. "They hate her because she is chosen/And has not denied Jesus' name." The other churches want to lower the standards of the speckled bird, watching her every move and trying to find fault with what she teaches.

The singer is glad he has found the speckled bird, who will bear him on her wings to meet Christ. The attitude in this song, which sets the purity of the bird—however speckled—against the liberal churches that desire to lower standards and deny Jesus' name, is understandable in the context of its biblical text (especially in the King James translation targeting pastors): "Mine heritage is unto me as a speckled bird, the birds round about are against her; come ye, assemble all the beasts of the field, come to devour. Many pastors have destroyed my vineyard, they have trodden my portion under foot, they have made my pleasant portion a desolate wilderness" (Jer. 12:9–10).

Most of the churches in country music are old country churches. For example, we have "The Church in the Wildwood" (William S. Pitts), "The Little White Church" (Mac Wiseman, Bobby Osborne), and at least three songs with the title "The Old Country Church." These are the churches where one gets saved. The old country church is often described as the place where the singer came to the Lord.

In the Louvin Brothers' "The Kneeling Drunkard's Plea," recorded recently by Johnny Cash, the singer sees the drunkard "stagger and lurch," falling down to pray before his mother's grave, but this all takes place "by an old country church."

A favorite in the bluegrass repertoire (where many of these songs can still be heard) is "River of Jordan," an old country gospel song about baptism: "Let the cool waters cleanse my soul." There is first a stanza about Jesus getting baptized in the Jordan by John the Baptist, then an exercise in Old Testament

typology, with an account of Namaan the Leper finding heal-
ing in the Jordan. The biblical waters then become manifested
in the singer's local church:

> The River of Jordan is many miles away
> That mighty river I may never see,
> But I'll find myself an altar in an old-fashioned church
> My river of Jordan that will be.

Not just a church, but an old-fashioned church.

Me and Jesus

Certainly, much of the appeal of the country church is nostalgia. Often the church is cast as a memory, with references to
mother, family, friends, and the sense of community in those
old times—all of which have usually passed away. "Little Brown
Church," an old tune that became a staple of Flatt and Scruggs,
is representative:

> I can see my Mother kneeling there
> As she talked to Jesus in earnest prayer
> When we were worried, we carried our load
> To the little brown church in the wide oak grove.

Here we have mother, Jesus, and a small church located in the
woods.

> I am thinking of the days that used to be
> And old friends that meant the world to me.
> On each Sunday morning we would go
> To the little brown church in the wide oak grove.

Not only does the little brown church conjure up a nostalgic
memory of family, friends, and childhood, the final stanza
establishes a sense of utter finality and loss: "It's so sad now
they have closed the doors to the little brown church in the wide
oak grove."

A church that has been closed down, along with the old-fashioned spirituality it embodied, is the subject of "That Little Old Country Church House" (written and recorded by the Masters Family, recorded also by Flatt and Scruggs). The old church where so many souls were saved is now locked up. The pulpit is covered with dust. The singer used to go to that church with his family and meet with his friends and listen to the preaching of old time religion. "The church is all forsaken and the people have turned away."

This goes beyond nostalgia. It is not just that time has passed, that the people are no longer there. Rather, "the people have turned away." The loss of the old-time religion is a matter of apostasy. The Bible prophesies that people will turn away from God and the true church. But the song ends with a non-churchly gospel invitation. Jesus saves, "and I know if you open up your heart, He will come within." The song is prophetic. In contemporary country music, the church as the place of salvation has all but disappeared.

Part of the reason for this disappearance is suggested in the previous song. Even though the church is closed, you can still "open up your heart" to Jesus. You do not really need a church to do that. A theological criticism of the old-time religion is that its emphasis on a direct, inner, personal relationship with God meant, in practice, a highly privatized faith—one that did not, in principle, need the mediation of the church. Harold Bloom argues in *The American Religion* that this subjectivism is characteristic of the distinctly American approach to religion—which according to Bloom is not Christianity at all but Gnosticism.[1] There can be no better illustration of Bloom's thesis than Tom T. Hall's "Me and Jesus," which he both wrote and performed. "Me and Jesus, got our own thing goin'," he claims. The two of them have it all worked out. And "we don't need anybody to tell us what it's all about."

Not that churches are absent in contemporary country music. They are often referred to as the place where weddings take place, as in Reba McIntire's "I'd Rather Ride Around with You" (Mark D. Sanders, Tim Nichols) or Shenandoah's hit "Church on Cumberland Road" (Bob Dipiero, Dennis Robbins, John Scott Sherrill), a country version of "Get Me to the Church on Time." (Again, the church they are frantically trying to drive to is somewhere out in the country.) Or after a marital breakup, a spouse wistfully recalls or drives by the church where the couple was married, as in Tracy Byrd's "Put Your Hand in Mine" (Skip Ewing, Jimmy Wayne Barber).

The stock of ministers has also gone down. Today they are often satirized, as the snake-handling paranoid preacher in Diamond Rio's "It's All in Your Head" (Tony Martin, Van Stephenson, Reese Wilson), or portrayed as succumbing to sexual temptations, as in Travis Tritt's "Bible Belt." Preachers on the radio or TV are presented as being interested only in getting donations (Mary-Chapin Carpenter's "I'll Take My Chances"; Charlie Daniels' "Long Haired Country Boy").

And yet, in the more heartwrenching songs—songs about struggles with alcoholism or songs about death—ministers do assume their role as spiritual mentors. In Collin Raye's "Little Rock" (Tom Douglas) an alcoholic calls his estranged wife about his progress, which includes getting involved with a church. "I haven't had a drink in 19 days," he tells her, and "I like the preacher from the Church of Christ."

Vince Gill's tribute on the death of his banjo-playing father, "The Key to Life," speaks of a minister's empathy and Christ-centered faith, with which the singer is in full agreement, despite his sorrow. "And when he died the preacher cried and said he's the lucky one/He's walkin' hand in hand with God's only son." Gill knows that what the preacher says is true, even though he'd love to hear his father play the banjo again.

It is evident that many country music songwriters and performers do, in fact, go to church. They present it casually, as a part of life. Quite a few love songs have church as their settings. In Ricochet's "Daddy's Money" (Bob Dipiero, Steve Seskin, Mark Sanders), the singer "can't concentrate on the preacher preachin'" because of that "angel singin' up there in the choir loft." In Sammy Kershaw's humorous "Vidalia" (Tim Nichols, Mark Sanders), a boy meets the feisty girl with the funny name • 93 in Sunday school. When someone snickered at the fact that she was named after an onion, "You laid the word of God/Up 'side of his head."

Then there is "God Will" by Lyle Lovett. Lyle's family were founding members of Trinity Lutheran Church in Klein, Texas (a fact he underscores in his web biography), and Lyle made a point of flying his pastor to Indiana to officiate at his wedding with Julia Roberts. Lovett's Lutheran background may be reflected—in his characteristically quirky, ironic way—in "God Will," which asks the musical question, Who will always forgive you, despite all of the rotten things you keep doing? The answer: "God will/But I won't." This, the song says, is the difference between him and God. Of course, Lutherans know they are supposed to forgive as they have been forgiven, but "God Will" wittily contrasts the radical grace of God with the pettiness of human sin. The song also gets across, in a humorous way, as Lutheran theology does in a rigorous theological way, the otherness of God. That is to say, a Lutheran could never have written "Me and Jesus."

In Lovett's even more humorous "Church," he describes an (un-Lutheran) fire-and-brimstone service, in which the preacher sermonizes past his time, so that the whole congregation is getting hungrier and hungrier. Finally, something mystical happens. The preacher stops preaching and a hush fills the church. "And then a great white dove from up above" descends to the pulpit. A fork appears in the preacher's hand. And the preacher—as hungry as everyone else—"ate that bird right there and then." The lines recall Luther's own lampoon of "enthusiast" preachers, who, he said, swallow the Holy Ghost, feathers and all. Though Lovett describes a fundamentalist-type service with humor, but also with sympathy and no malice, the song demonstrates his Lutheran background: in the narrative, a boy, scheming to make the pastor finish his sermon, climbs up to the choir loft in the balcony, which is where Lutheran churches tend to place the choir—out of sight, unlike the Baptist-type choir right in front, which proved so distracting in Ricochet's "Daddy's Money."

94 •

The figure of the preacher, however battered, shows up with new dignity in Garth Brooks' "Fit for a King" (Jim Rushing, Carl Jackson). This preacher is not exactly the leader of a church—he harangues people from a street corner. Nor is he a paragon of conventional righteousness—he is an alcoholic. He is homeless, dressed in rags, dirty. Though he is preaching fire and brimstone at the passing cars, he is offering salvation through the Savior. Though this kind of street preaching is open to ridicule, this particular preacher, in spite of being a down-and-out drunk, speaks with an authority born out of his own struggles. Pointing to the Bible, he says, "I'm proof that the good Lord/Can save any man."

The song, having established an interesting spiritual point, seems to shift its focus to the external by concentrating on his homelessness, specifically, his ratty clothing. In heaven, his rags will be changed to clothes fit for a king. But the most salient lines tell us what gives this street evangelist his authenticity: "His grip on the gospel" is "his one claim to fame."

The Country Virtues

Though the country church is no longer the potent presence it once was, though the "church" has been downgraded, the "country" part remains as the embodiment of virtue and even true religion. There are few more consistent or predictable themes in country music than the moral and spiritual superiority of rural life over that of the big city.

The cultural rivalry between the country and the city is long-standing in country music. An excellent example of this rivalry is found in "A Country Boy Can Survive," by Hank Williams Jr. (reprised by Chad Brock in the fall of 1999 for the Y2K scare). The singer contemplates how, if civilization falls (a secular apocalypse), those who know how to plant, set trotlines, skin a buck, and have "a rifle, a shotgun, and a four-wheel drive" will survive. But there is more to it than that: here in the country "we say grace, and we say ma'am"; the city is not only a place of soft dependence, it is also a place of evil and danger: •95

> I had a good friend in New York City
> He never called me by my name just HillBilly
> My Grandpa taught me to live off the land
> And his taught him to be a business man
> He used to send me pictures of the Broadway Night
> And I'd send him some homemade wine
> But he was killed by a man with a switchblade knife
> For forty-three dollars my friend lost his life
> I'd love to spit some Beechnut in that dude's eye
> And shoot him with my ole .45
> 'Cause a country boy can survive
> Country folks can survive.

And yet survival, in the face of the encroachment of the city and all that it represents, is not easy. Some recent songs, such as Junior Brown's "Don't Sell the Farm," are about country families struggling to maintain their way of life against urbanization and economic pressures. Montgomery Gentry's "Daddy Won't Sell the Farm" (Steve Fox, Robin Branden) is a story about a strong father who raises his family on his land, only to have it threatened by developers. He does not back down. "He's going to live and die in the eye of an urban storm." And when his boy, the singer, inherits the place (which is precisely when many family farms get sold off), he vows to raise his own family in the same way. His children can have the security of knowing that their own "daddy won't sell the farm."

The plight of the family farmer has given rise to a yearly event in country music, Willie Nelson's Farm-Aid concert, a big outdoor festival whose proceeds benefit farmers in danger of losing their land. At one of these concerts, Nelson teamed up with Bob Dylan to write "Heartland," which puts into words both the economic plight and the spiritual trauma represented by the loss of one's country home. As bankers take away his home and land, "There's a big gaping hole in my chest now, where my heart was." But more than that, the loss of the farm shakes his faith. There is "a hole in the sky, where God used to be."

To be sure, there are songs making fun of country naïveté (Jo Dee Messina's "You're Not in Kansas Anymore" [Zack Turner,

Tim Nichols]), and there are a number of songs about the yearning of young people to escape their narrow little communities for the wide-open world outside. Actually, the stifling places in such songs tend to be small towns, not small farms. Thus we have Hal Ketchum's "Small Town Saturday Night" (Patrick Alger, Henry DeVito), with its evocative imagery of aimless young people getting in trouble because there is nothing else to do and its pointed cosmology: "Lucy, you know the world must be flat/'Cause when people leave town, they never come back."

In "Someday" by Steve Earle, a young man pumps gas for cars that drive by his dull town on the interstate, promising himself that "I'm gonna get out of here someday" and fantasizing about taking his '67 Chevy on the interstate and never looking back.

Perhaps even more common is the theme of leaving home for the big city, but later regretting it and wanting to come back. This secularized version of the parable of the prodigal son is best summed up in Alabama's hit "Down Home" (Rick Bowles, Josh Lea): "When I was a boy I couldn't wait to leave this place. But now I wanna see my children raised down home." Or as Neal McCoy puts it in the title of his song, "The City Put the Country Back in Me" (Geiger, Mullis, Huffman).

More eloquent is the Dixie Chicks' "Cowboy Take Me Away" (Martie Seidel, Marcus Hummon) about the yearning to escape the crowds and the big buildings of the city. The singer dreams of a cowboy taking her away to a Texas landscape of bluebonnets, open sky, and farmer's soil. This liberation from the city is in terms of both love and religion. "Set me free, Oh, I pray,/Closer to Heaven above and closer to you."

In "Where Corn Don't Grow," recorded by both Travis Tritt and Waylon Jennings (Roger Murrah, Mark Allan), a seventeen-year-old smart aleck hurts the feelings of his father by talking about dreams of a life "where corn don't grow." Once he leaves the farm and goes to the city, he finds that it is very different from what he had dreamed: "I can't say he didn't tell me this city life's a hard row to hoe/It's funny how a dream can turn around, where corn don't grow."

The prodigal son figure is played out explicitly in Travis Tritt's video, which shows the young man going off to the big city, whereupon he loses everything, turns to crime, and gets arrested. In the last scene, he is shown getting off a bus, walking up to his father, still on the old front porch, where they embrace in a tearful reunion.

If the country represents virtue, the city represents vice. To be sure, one often wants to break away from virtue and to experience the pleasures of vice. But in the long run, the city and its allures only bring heartache and loneliness. This is the theme of Bill Anderson's "City Lights," recorded by Ray Price:

> A bright array of city lights, as far as I can see,
> The great white wave shines through the night,
> on lonely guys like me.
> The cabarets and honky tonks,
> Their flashing signs invite,
> The broken heart to lose itself,
> In the glow of city lights. . . .
>
> They paint a pretty picture,
> of a world that's gay and bright,
> But it's just a mask for loneliness,
> Behind those city lights.

This song makes the interesting point that God made the natural world of the country, but man made the city, whose bright lights and pleasures are nothing more than evasions:

> The world was dark and God made stars,
> to brighten up the night,
> But God who put the stars above,
> I don't believe made those lights.
>
> For it's just a place for men to cry,
> when things don't turn out right,
> Just a place to run away and hide,
> behind those city lights.

Interestingly, these same sentiments—developed also in Merle Haggard's "Big City" (with Dean Holloway)—are echoed by the refugees of the rock and folk scenes who, to one degree or another, have "gone country." Perhaps the most harrowing and apocalyptic interpretation of the urban landscape is "Sin City" by Gram Parsons, who led many veterans of the sixties rock scene to the discovery of country music. The city, he warns, is full of sin. City life is all about money, getting it, spending it, and going into debt. Behind it all, Satan is looming. Nothing is secure, with the whole financial edifice threatening to crumble. The whole town is insane. And all the skyscrapers and wealth cannot shield anyone from God's judgment: "On the thirty-first floor, a gold painted door/Won't keep out the Lord's burning rain."

The song combines images of high finance and California earthquake fears with warnings against Satan and the prospect of God's Gomorah-like judgment. In contrast to this urban nightmare, Parsons wrote "Hickory Wind," which harks back to the old songs of memory, home, and the consolations of nature:

> In South Carolina there are many tall pines
> I remember the oak tree that we used to climb
> But now when I'm lonesome, I always pretend
> That I'm getting the feel of hickory wind.
>
> I started out younger at most everything
> All the riches and pleasures, what else could life bring?
> But it makes me feel better each time it begins
> Callin' me home, hickory wind.

Similarly, Buffy Sainte-Marie, who made her career in the sixties' folk scene, sings about turning her back on the city in "I'm Going to Be a Country Girl Again." As the rain falls on the buildings and cars of the city, she leaves behind the bars, department stores, and big city friends. She wants to be a country girl again. The Broadway lights cannot compare to a green field. Going to college and getting a good education does not erase her yearning for the country: "I've spent my time in study, •99 oh I've taken my degree, . . . But what I've learned came long ago, and not from such as these."

Lucinda Williams, in her "Sidewalks of the City," does not escape to the country, but finds the city heartless and unsettling, with its decaying buildings, graffiti, sirens, and human hunger. She calls for a human relationship, a yearning she describes in theological language: "Hold me, baby, give me some faith . . . /Give me love, give me grace." The dismal images of the city make her call out, in a secularized way, for security, love, grace, and faith.

The Pilgrimage

The last major motif of the old country gospel songs, as cited by Ronnie Pugh, is life as a pilgrimage. "This World Is Not My Home," as one title puts it, "I'm just a-passing through." Life is depicted as a journey. After many trials, tribulations, and other stops along the way, one can arrive at the final destination, namely, heaven. Old songs that are still part of the bluegrass repertoire present the theme directly, as in "Heaven's Bright Shore" and "In Heaven We'll Never Grow Old." More recently, country artists writing in this tradition have added "A Beautiful Life" (Bill Monroe) and "Your Long Journey" (Doc Watson). The classic exposition is "I Am a Pilgrim" by the pioneering country guitar player Merle Travis. "I am a pilgrim and a stranger," he sings, "Travelling through this wearisome land." But his journey has a destination, his true home, a city not made by hands (an echo of 2 Corinthians 5:1).

Ronnie Pugh points to several early songs that update the pilgrim motif in terms of the new means of transportation. "Life Is Like a Mountain Railroad," "This Train Is Bound for Glory," and the oft-recorded (including by Patsy Cline) "Life's Railway to Heaven," among others, use the metaphor of a train. "I'm Usin' My Bible for a Roadmap" uses the metaphor of an automobile.

Hank Williams did a number of pilgrimage songs, including ones hinging on trains and highways, using traveling and rambling as images for life. The very name of his group was "The

Drifting Cowboys," and his other persona was "Luke the *Drifter.*" In songs like "Ramblin' Man," "The Devil's Train," and "Lost Highway" (Leon Payne), he takes the figure of life as a pilgrimage about as far as it can go.

Traveling, in all of its guises, is a constant theme in country music, with its train songs, car songs, truck-driving songs. Then there are the songs about hobos, men who can't be tied down, travelers through life who can say with Hank Snow, in his great catalog of American places, "I've Been Everywhere, Man" (Geoff Mack). It might be stretching it to see all of this traveling as variations on the pilgrimage, but certainly the traces are there.

Among alternative country artists—those too serious or too complex for the radio—the pilgrimage motif remains popular. In Steve Earle's "Nowhere Road," he complains that "I been down this road just searchin' for the end," but "it don't go nowhere." He hears rumors of a destination, but he has no idea what it is.

Another alternative country artist, Ray Wylie Hubbard, in "Dangerous Spirits," evokes a mysterious and menacing gunfighter who thought he was both above the law and outside of grace. But eventually "I let my revolver fall from my hands/and put on the coat of a pilgrim." In part, his change comes from meeting and loving a woman who prays to a loving God.

The old songs of pilgrimage—which stress the transitory nature of life under the prospect of eternity—continue to have a strong resonance, as evident in a telling cross-generational collaboration. Randy Scruggs, son of bluegrass legend Earl Scruggs, wrote a song with Johnny Cash, entitled "Passin' Thru." On his album *Crown of Jewels*, Randy performed the song with alternative rock star Joan Osborne. The old imagery, set to a dark and driving bass line, is brought back to life in the contemporary imagination:

> I have stood upon the mountain
> I have seen the other side
> I have wrestled with the devil
> I have wrestled with my pride
> I have been down in the valley

> I have stood out in the rain
> I have seen my love forsaken
> Felt the pleasure and the pain

The catalog of life's experiences goes on, with tears of sadness and tears of joy, and an account of having turned away from "lyin', prejudice, and greed" and finding "the peace within the noise." The refrain, though, is pilgrimage:

> There's one thing that's for certain
> One chord that rings true
> It's a mighty world we live in
> But the truth is, we're only passin' thru.

Sometimes the refrain changes one word: "It's a *wicked* world we live in." The combination of Scruggs' Bob Dylan–style voice, plus Joan Osborne's emotionally searing sound—all at the service of Johnny Cash's gospel traditionalism—makes for a riveting performance and an utterly convincing repristination of the country gospel tradition.

7

Country Music's Moral Tradition

MARRIAGE AND D-I-V-O-R-C-E

Focusing on the religious dimension of country music as we are doing by no means is meant to imply that country music is particularly pious or even moral. Country music does have a place for Christianity; it does tend to be culturally conservative. But country is also the music of redneck hell-raising. The family is often celebrated, but other major themes in country music include adultery and divorce. If country is the music of rural America, it is also the music of honky-tonks, with their neon signs, "loose women," and maudlin drunks. Sex may be even more prominent in country music than in rock and roll. On the other hand, it is often marital sex that is sung about. There is certainly more alcohol pouring through country songs than there are drugs in rock—and many country stars have been both alcoholics *and* drug addicts.

Country music is filled with conflicts, primarily because it presents adult life—with all of the adult problems—with a great deal of honesty and realism. To speak of realism, of course, can beg the question of what one considers to be real. The world of country music, even at its rowdiest, has been shaped by the Christian worldview. As Ira Louvin put it, "God is real, but Satan is real too" (in his recitation to "Satan Is Real"). We need God's grace because we are desperate sinners, and sin is not merely a moral transgression but the weakness bound up in the human condition.

There are two genres of American music that concern themselves largely with suffering: the blues and country music. American culture tends, on the whole, to be success oriented and optimistic, but these two related genres—growing out of the experiences of poor Southern blacks and poor Southern whites, respectively—embrace loss, failure, and emotional devastation.

People who dislike country music tend to complain that it is depressing. Their stereotype of a country song—both of the content of the music and the person who is listening to it—centers around a down-and-out hayseed on a barstool drinking himself into oblivion because his woman has left him. Indeed, there is some truth to the stereotype. In his paean to country music, "Don't Rock the Jukebox," Alan Jackson's character says that he doesn't have anything against rock and roll, but he's too heartbroken for that kind of music. "I've been down and lonely/ Ever since she's left." He needs to hear a country song.

Vince Gill uses the very same setting, with a bereft man requesting that only country music be played on the jukebox, in his "Kindly Keep It Country." Because he is feeling lonely, he asks for a sad song. To a melancholy but infectious melody, with a weeping steel guitar, Gill strikes at a strong element of the country music aesthetic: "I love to hear 'em sing about the misery and pain." This is the pleasure of tragedy—the Louvin Brothers recorded an album called *Tragic Songs of Life*—complete with the tragic flaws of humanity and the catharsis of fear and pity. But as the ancients always pointed out, there can be no tragedy without a moral order.

Drinking songs and cheatin' songs are nearly always guilt-ridden and full of regret, loss, and self-accusation. That is to say, they are secular songs of repentance. They are thus complementary to the constantly repeated country music ideals of love, marriage, and family—the only antidotes to the unbearable pain of "lonesomeness."

Love Songs

Nearly all popular music consists of love songs. Rock songs, pop songs, jazz, blues, folk ballads, and operas have as their most frequent subject the passion and joy and pain of love. They depict men and women falling in love with each other, the ups and downs of courtship, the complexities of human relationships, the anguish of broken or unrequited love, the satisfactions of marriage. Country music is no different. Nearly every song on country radio, nearly every cut on every album, has something to do with the love between a man and a woman.

The flip side of love, however, is loneliness—the feeling that one is not loved or has no one to love. When love has been lost, the relationship broken or tossed away, this feeling is heightened almost past endurance. The emotion of loneliness is what country music expresses with its greatest eloquence—a notable example being Hank Williams' song "I'm So Lonesome, I Could Cry." Loneliness animates songs about drinking, divorce, and other negative topics in country music. In such songs, the loss of love is often the consequence of one's own bad behavior, which only intensifies the feeling of desolation. And loneliness healed—the sense of loving and being loved—is the theme of marriage songs and family songs, in all of their sentimental nostalgia and veneration for the home. It is the theme of the religious songs too, the phenomenon of being loved by God, even though it isn't deserved, a love manifested in other kinds of love as well, all of them being God's provision to ease the human being's cosmic loneliness.

Admittedly, the portrayal of sex in country music is often crude and salacious. Women are sometimes portrayed as sex objects to be ogled, not only in contemporary songs like Neal McCoy's "The Shake" (Jon McElroy, Butch Carr) but in more traditional songs like Conway Twitty's "Tight Fittin' Jeans" (Mike Huffman) and Little Jimmy Dickens' "Geraldine" (about watching a nearly nude sunbather). There are innumerable songs about "honky-tonk angels" and picking up women in bars, such as Earl Conley's "Heavenly Bodies" and "Little Less Talk and a Lot More Action" (Jimmy Stewart, Keith Hinton), recorded by both Hank Williams Jr. and Toby Keith. Sammy Kershaw had a hit with "Third Rate Romance" (Russell Smith), about an impersonal one-night stand in a cheap hotel. Garth Brooks and Deana Carter both had hits about teenagers losing their virginity, in "That Summer" (Pat Alger, Sandy Mahl, Garth Brooks) and "Strawberry Wine" (Matraca Berg, Gary Harrison), respectively. Patty Loveless sang about extramarital sex on the rebound, with "Lonely Too Long" (Mike Lawler, Bill Rice, Sharon Rice): "We ain't done nothin' wrong/We just been lonely too long." In this song, sex is an escape from loneliness.

Little or no love is depicted in these crude songs—just sex. But when country music does depict love, it nearly always points to marriage. This is true even of light, humorous songs about young love, such as Joe Diffie's "John Deere Greene" (Dennis Linde), about using tractor paint on the water tower to inscribe "Billy Bob loves Charlene," a pledge that is visible long after the two are married. Marriage is also anticipated in Kenny Chesney's self-explanatory "She Thinks My Tractor's Sexy" (Jim Collins, Paul Overstreet).

An increasingly common motif in country music is to follow a couple from childhood, through courtship and marriage, to having children of their own. George Strait's "Check Yes or No" (Danny A. Wells, Dana Hunt Oglesby) and Clay Walker's "One, Two, I Love You" (Bucky Jones, Ed Hill) both begin with nostalgic memories of a little boy and a little girl playing together and end with them as grown-up husband and wife. The latter song, along with Tim McGraw's tearjerker "Don't Take the Girl"

(Craig Martin, Larry W. Johnson), takes the couple all the way to the birth of their own child, whereupon the cycle of life is complete. In all of these songs, the love between a man and a woman is presented as part of a bigger scheme—the forming of a family—as children grow up, fall in love, get married, and become parents of a new generation of children, who themselves will follow the same pattern.

One of the most eloquent of these life-cycle songs is Trisha Yearwood's "She's in Love with the Boy" (Jon Ims). It is a detailed narrative of Katie, a bored farmgirl, who goes out with her boyfriend Tommy in his "beat-up Chevy truck." Her daddy—the strong, protective, and strict father common to country music—does not approve. "He ain't worth a lick," he insists. "When it came to brains, he got the short end of the stick. . . . But Katie's young and, man, she just don't care/She'd follow Tommy anywhere." The song follows the two as they go to the drive-in ("They're too busy holding on to one another/To even care about the show"), and then to the Tastee Freeze, where Tommy gives her his high school ring, which "will have to do/Till I can buy a wedding band." The song, strongly evocative of small-town, rural life, continues as Katie tries to sneak into the house, only to find her daddy waiting on them both:

> Her daddy's waiting up till half past twelve,
> When they come sneaking up the walk.
> He says, "young lady get on up to your room
> While me and junior have a talk."

The father's words establish both teenagers as children, and he will by no means let this boy who "ain't worth a lick" have anything to do with his daughter. But then we hear from someone who has been silent in the course of the narrative—the mother:

> But Mama breaks in and says, "Don't lose your temper.
> It wasn't very long ago
> When you yourself was just a hay-seed plowboy
> Who didn't have a row to hoe.

My daddy said you wasn't worth a lick
When it came to brains, you had the short end of the stick
But he was wrong and, honey, you are too
Katie looks at Tommy like I still look at you."

The love of the children is just a reprise of the love of the parents. What her husband says about Tommy is the same thing people said about him when he was Tommy's age. And the mother is just like Katie: "She's in love with the boy." The song, far from vilifying the strict father in opposition to young love—as one might expect from a melodrama or rock song—ends up affirming the love the mother and father have for each other, which helps them understand and identify with their daughter. Since "she's gonna marry that boy someday," the generational cycle will continue.

If the focus of love in rock and roll is the boyfriend or girlfriend, the focus of love in country music—whether yearned for, fulfilled, or lost—is the spouse. True, the stereotype of the restrictive, henpecking wife appears, though always in humorous songs, such as Collin Raye's "That's My Story (and I'm Stickin' to It)" (Lee Roy Parnell, Tony Haselden, C. Alex Hawkins), Junior Brown's "My Wife Thinks You're Dead," and Vince Gill's "One More Last Chance," about a hapless husband whose wife took his glasses so he can't drive to the bars, going there anyway, chugging along on his John Deere tractor. But a good number of the love ballads that have been a staple of country music, from Jim Reeves to John Michael Montgomery, have been about married love. Then there are outright paeans to marriage, such as Kathy Mattea's "Eighteen Wheels and a Dozen Roses" (Paul Nelson, Gene Nelson) about a trucker who retires so that "he can spend the rest of his life with the one that he loves."

Country music's frank treatment of sexual relations includes the awareness—strangely missing from much of pop culture—that the primary locus of sex is within marriage. Certainly even marital sex is sometimes portrayed crudely, as in Trace Adkins' "I Left Something Turned On at Home" (Billy Lawson, John Schweers); but it is treated with tasteful sensuality in classic songs like Charlie Pride's "Kiss an Angel Good Morning" (Ben Peters) and Charlie Rich's "Behind Closed Doors" (K. O'Dell). Both of these songs portray the wife as embodying two distinct roles at the same time: the virtuous, respectable, civilizing lady and the passionate, desirable lover.

Love songs from a wife to her husband tend to focus on her feeling of being accepted, her sense of security, and her appreciation of the comfortable intimacies of the couple's everyday life. Martina McBride's "My Baby Loves Me" (Gretchen Peters) is telling. She doesn't need fashion magazines. She doesn't have to dress like a beauty queen. It doesn't matter whether she wears high heels or sneakers. "My baby loves me just the way that I am." What the wife is grateful for—in contrast to the pressures women feel from the cultural definitions of beauty, as expressed in the fashion industry and in the dating game—is her husband's acceptance of who she is. The song sums it up in language that may be borrowed from pop psychology but that has also been used as a description of God's love, the *agape* that is the biblical model for how human beings too are to love one another: He "gives me unconditional love."

Trisha Yearwood describes "Perfect Love" in a song of that title (Stephany Smith, Sunny Russ) not in terms of some lofty ideal, as one might expect with talk of perfection. Rather, perfect love involves reading the newspaper together, drinking coffee and talking, stopping by to see the in-laws, driving around, going for walks. "When you look at me the way you do,/I can't help but look right back at you." In the context of ordinary life, that direct looking at each other is what genuine love, as known only in marriage, is all about. They are not trying to make history, the song says, as in the grandiose (and generally doomed) romances of tragedies and melodramas. But the everyday life they have together constitutes a perfect love.

Love songs from a husband to his wife are often unabashed expressions of gratitude for her putting up with him. A good example is Radney Foster's "Anyone Else," made into a hit by Collin Raye: "Anyone else would've been long gone . . . And not a soul would blame you after what I put you through." And yet, •109 unaccountably, she stays with him. This is the male equivalent of the craving for unconditional love.

One problem for couples, according to the song, is "Too much grindstone, too little time with you." In contemporary country songs such as these, the pressures and demands of work prevent married couples from spending time together. Monte Warden's "I Wanna Know Her Again" is about a man's desire to get reacquainted with his wife. He has been doing well at work, and the company has big plans for him. But what does that matter if he's too busy to spend time with his wife? He wants to know her again, he sings in the chorus, "Find out how she's been/And then hold her tight."

Another motif in songs from a husband to his wife is a promise to love her forever, looking forward to an old age together. In John Michael Montgomery's "I Swear" (Frank J. Myers, Gary Baker), a husband, reprising his wedding vows, promises that he will never leave his wife:

> I swear, by the moon and the stars in the sky
> I'll be there
> I swear, like a shadow that's by your side
> I'll be there
> For better or worse, 'til death do us part
> I'll love you with every beat of my heart
> I swear

The singer swears that this vow will hold true even when they get old. "When there's silver in your hair/You won't have to ask if I still care," he tells her, "'cause as time turns the page, my love won't age at all."

A particularly charming rendition of the same idea, with a rather inarticulate husband reassuring his wife of his love, is Randy Travis' "Forever and Ever, Amen" (Don Schlitz, Paul Overstreet). The singer acknowledges that time takes its toll, turning brown hair gray. "But honey, I don't care, I'm not in love with your hair." He would love her even if her hair fell out. The refrain describes old men sitting around discussing the weather and old women discussing old men, a future embraced in the repeated promise of faithfulness: "I'm gonna love you forever, forever and ever, Amen."

The religious language in this song recalls how love songs from husbands often include a recognition that the wife is a gift from God. This has been seen with Tracy Byrd's tipping his hat to "The Keeper of the Stars," and Garth Brooks' "Unanswered Prayers." Vince Gill's "My Kind of Woman/My Kind of Man," recorded as a duet with Patty Loveless, brings all of these motifs together: commitment, contentment, permanence, and passion. The couple's compatibility and their relationship is God's work: "A match made in Heaven/By God's gentle hand."

Two hit songs recorded by Clint Black are essentially meditations on the wedding service. "Something That We Do" (written with Skip Ewing) begins with a memory of a couple's wedding and goes on to reflect at length on the nature of love. The union of marriage is such "that we can't tell where I end and where you start." The song's point, expressed in the refrain, is that love is not a passive condition but a mutual action. *Falling in love* and *being in love* are the romantic conventions; but married couples realize that love is "something that we do." In a similar song, "When I Said I Do," recorded by Black with his wife (television personality Lisa Hartman), the couple examine the meaning of their marriage vows: When they said "I do," they vowed to be faithful forever. The couple goes on to reflect on change, the ups and downs of life, and the permanence of their union: "Only you and I can undo all that we became/That makes us so much more than a woman and a man."

In marriage, a separate man and a separate woman become something more than the sum of their parts; they become, as Scripture says, one flesh. The song makes a strong statement about the marital union. And yet, in the very words that express it, there is a startling loophole: "Only you and I can undo all that we became." The song first echoes and then violates Christ's teaching that in marriage the man and woman become one flesh and that what God has joined together must not be put asunder (see Matt. 19:4–6). The union can be broken after all, and the husband and the wife are the ones who can undo their marriage. This opens up another major theme of country music: divorce.

D-I-V-O-R-C-E

One of the most common subjects of country songs—whether folk tunes, ballads, dance numbers, or humorous novelty songs—is being left by the one you love. Not all of the lost-love songs are explicitly about divorce, since being dumped before marriage is part and parcel of the courting game, but a good many of the broken-heart songs allude to "leaving" and the end of long-term relationships. "She's Gone, Gone, Gone," sang Lefty Frizzell (Harlan Howard). "Faded Love," a poignant tune about the gradual death of a relationship, was written by Bob Wills and became one of his most beloved songs, a classic in the fiddle repertoire and a hit by Patsy Cline. Tammy Wynette coyly spelled out "D-I-V-O-R-C-E" in her song so the child wouldn't know, but this was nothing new to country music fans. They knew that the figure of the fool on the barstool, drowning his sorrows in that whiskey river and listening to sad songs on the jukebox, is nearly always a casualty of a broken marriage.

Why are there so many songs like this, given the high view of marriage that is evident in country music? Long before divorce became commonplace in middle-class America, it afflicted the poor and working classes, particularly in the rural South. Even today, the so-called Bible Belt has the nation's highest divorce rate, leading some pundits to speculate that there must be a correlation between getting a divorce and being Baptist. This is not fair. Sociologists point out that income and social class are what determine divorce rates. Two groups have the highest rate of failed marriages: the very poor and the very rich. Why this should be the case is not clear. Not having much money can put a strain on any marriage, and having lots of money may mean there is less at stake. The poor and the rich may have the cultural habit of being relatively unrestrained in their passions, compared to the more orderly and controlled lives of the middle class. Who knows what the reasons are? But even A. P. and Sara Carter, for all their songs of faith and family, could not keep their marriage together.

It is important to realize, though, that the songs about leaving by no means contradict the songs about marriage, which emphasize the importance of marital unity. The songs about leaving, with very few exceptions, are songs full of regret, expressing a sense of unbearable loss and emotional devastation. True, there are humorous treatments of the subject, such as Mark Chesnutt's "Going Thru the Big D (and I Don't Mean Dallas)" (Ronnie Rogers, Jon Wright, Mark Wright) and George Strait's "All My Ex's Live in Texas" (Sanger D. Shafer, Lyndia J. Shafer), but even these have a subtext of misery. The leaving songs are the shadow side of marriage songs: the bond between a man and a woman is so absolute that, when it is broken, they—to draw on another Patsy Cline song—"fall to pieces."

No one can convey feminine anguish like Reba McIntire. In "For My Broken Heart" (Liz Hengber, Keith Palmer), the song describes a man's departure and a woman's first night alone:

> There were no angry words at all
> As we carried boxes down the hall.
> One by one we put them in your car
> Nothing much for us to say,
> One last goodbye and you drove away.

The practical details of packing up, the lack now of any arguments, the ordinariness of the scene, all add to the poignancy. She can't bring herself to sleep in their bed, so she sleeps on the couch instead. In the refrain, she brings God into it: "Last night I prayed the Lord my soul to keep,/Then I cried myself to sleep." The next morning—"The first of many lonely mornings I have to face"—she fixes coffee, her ex thoughtfully calls her to see how she is, the day goes on, and she realizes "the world didn't stop for my broken heart."

The same setting—just after a man has packed up his things and left—is the occasion for Dolly Parton's plaintive performance of "Just When I Needed You Most" (Randy Van Warmer). The title describes when he left her, at the very time she needed him most. Again, the chorus brings God into her emotional turmoil: "Now where I'll find comfort/God knows."

Breakup songs from a woman's point of view are sometimes poignant laments like these, but sometimes they are self-help therapy: I am going to get through this. I didn't need him anyway. He'll be sorry now. Sometimes the songs are defiant. Sometimes they are witty put-downs of a no-good man. For example, there is Patty Loveless' version of "You Can Feel Bad If It Makes You Feel Better" (Matraca Berg, Tim Krekel). The setting is, once again, the same scene described by Reba McIntire and Dolly Parton: a man packing to leave. But the attitude is very different. The man apologizes for hurting her and assumes that she is falling apart. But she isn't. You can "picture me cryin' reading all your love letters" and "walkin' around in your old sweaters," but that isn't the way it is at all. She dismisses the man's protestations of remorse as fake, his alleged concern whether she is miserable and his emotionalism as mere self-pity, a little catharsis so he can feel better about leaving. It is clear that while he feels bad about leaving her for the pursuit of self-fulfillment, the woman here doesn't feel bad at all. Scorning him and mocking his phony emotions, she feels just fine that he's gone—and good riddance.

This in-your-face attitude—which can also be found in earlier country songs, by artists such as Loretta Lynn and Tammy Wynette—has been taken to a new level with the advent of feminism, whose influence even in country music testifies to its impact on contemporary American culture. In "You Can Feel Bad," it is the man who leaves to find himself, but increasingly, it is the woman who leaves, as in Lonestar's humorous "No News" (Hogin, Barnhart, Sanders). Presented from the viewpoint of a hapless male, the dim husband takes literally his wife's statement that their "romance has headed south," naively thinks she is simply on a long road trip, and can't understand why he hasn't heard from her. Martina McBride had a hit with the more maudlin "A Broken Wing" (James House, Sam Hogin, Phil Barnhart—it is interesting that this song was actually written by men), about a woman whose husband would "break her spirit down" and shoot down her dreams. "One Sunday morning she didn't go to church" (a significant transgression in this context); he went up to find her (apparently, he never went to church) and found that she had left through the window, so that she could, presumably, spread her broken wings.

More pensive is Reba McIntire's "Is There Life Out There?" (Susan Longacre, Rick Giles). She got married at twenty and now wonders about what she has missed. "Is there life out there," she wonders, "beyond her family and home?" To be sure, she really does not want to leave her husband and family, but in this mood, she wants to do something foolish—just for herself. Although not quite a divorce song, it does, however, articulate a dissatisfaction that a husband had better attend to. There are a number of songs from the viewpoint of clueless husbands, kicking themselves for missing the warning signs that their wives were unhappy (for example, Doug Stone's "Why Didn't I Think of That?" [Jim Glazer, C. Allen, J. Green] and Brooks and Dunn's "How Long Gone (Are You Gonna Be?)" [S. Camp, J. Sherrill]).

Then there is the overt feminism of Mary-Chapin Carpenter's "He Thinks He'll Keep Her." The title is taken from an old commercial that has a complacent husband saying these condescending words about his busy wife, expressing an attitude that even nonfeminists find offensive. The song presents the feminist stereotype of marriage as an institution of male dominance. Because she makes the coffee, makes the beds, and does the laundry, the husband, out of his sublime generosity, "thinks he'll keep her." The chorus interweaves images of domestic order with the smug male refrain—words not only of condescension but of ownership.

Yes, marriage, according to the song, is "safe," and even "benign." But the song questions the very concept of a perpetual commitment and lifelong vows. "She said forever," but what if "you'd change your mind?" Finally, she acts and walks out of the marriage. The songwriter is canny enough and real- • 115 istic enough, though, to realize that this will not be the answer either. The problem is not just with a particular husband or even with the institution of marriage. After fifteen years of marriage, with all of its hard work, she never got paid. Now she's getting minimum wage in the typing pool. The refrain is repeated—only this time, the order and hard work refer to the dead-end job with which she must now support herself, and "he thinks he'll keep her" is said by her boss. Women are victimized not just by individual men but by the whole economic superstructure of the society.

Mary-Chapin Carpenter, an extraordinarily talented singer and songwriter, was a Princeton graduate coming into country music from the highly educated middle class. "He Thinks He'll Keep Her" is far more radical than most country songs, though Reba McIntire from Chockie, Oklahoma, can be just as subversive.

A more conservative take on a wife's departure can be found in Patty Loveless' "You Don't Even Know Who I Am" (G. Peters). A woman suddenly leaves piled-up laundry, drops the kids off at her mother's, and walks out of her marriage. She leaves her wedding ring on the pillow and a note with the complaint: "You don't even know who I am. . . . So what do you care if I go?" The husband comes back to the empty house. He calls to apologize, though he does not know what for. He realizes that she's right. He goes to work every morning and comes home to her every night. And then the husband repeats her refrain: "And you don't even know who I am."

The song begins as a conventional complaint of an unhappy housewife, and the listener accepts it as such. But then there is a twist. It is not just that the husband hasn't taken time for his wife; she hasn't taken time for him either. The husband goes to work every day to provide for her and their children. He is faithful to her. To the country mind, those are no small things. But the self-absorbed wife has no interest in who *he* is. Their marriage is indeed in trouble—neither of them care—but it is too simplistic to blame one party only; both partners must share the responsibility for their relationship.

As Roger Miller says in "Husbands and Wives" (covered by Brooks and Dunn), marriages break up because of human pride and the lack of forgiveness. "It's my belief pride is the chief cause in the decline/In the number of husbands and wives." Country music may be the only musical genre that explores the relationship between men and women in an honest, realistic way, refusing—unlike most popular music—to idealize romantic love or to gloss over the difficulties of relationships, all the while affirming, even in the breach, the bonds of marriage.

Divorce songs from the man's point of view tend to be guilt-ridden meditations on what he has lost. Usually, the men are presented as emotional wrecks. The ex-wife, on the other hand, goes on with her life—finding someone new, raising their kids, pulling herself together, getting remarried. The ex-husband looks on, bereft and in despair. Or in the words of the Garth Brooks song, "She's Gonna Make It (but He Never Will)" (with Kent Blazy, Kim Williams). The song presents the point of view of a man who wanted out after being married seven years. But now after a mere seven months of freedom, he's falling apart. He watches his wife from a distance. She is getting on with her life. She is coping. She looks good in a new dress he has never seen before. Ironically, he knows that she would take him back. "But the fool in him that walked out/Is the fool who just won't ask." Again, it is his "foolish pride" (to use a title by Travis Tritt) that is the true barrier to love and reunion.

A man who has left his wife is often described as a fool—another common motif in country music. Sometimes the fool is a man who has been oblivious to the fact that his woman has been cheating on him (Dwight Yoakam's "The Heartaches of a Fool"), but more often the fool is the self-ascribed epithet for a man who has ruined his marriage. A clear statement of this theme is from George Strait, "Famous Last Words of a Fool" (Dean Dillin, Rex Huston). Those famous last words, as the chorus makes clear, are "You won't break my heart" and "I don't love you." The newly single man tries to rationalize—this will be easy; he can find someone else. But his heart is breaking as his last words to her echo in his mind. Strait's "Thoughts of a Fool" (Mel Tillis, Wayne P. Walker), Willie Nelson's "Heartaches of a Fool," Webb Pierce's "Memory #1" (Wayne Walker, Max Powell), and countless others—including a good many drinking songs—are variations of the fool's lament.

The anguish of losing one's family is another common motif in songs that focus on the feelings of ex-husbands. A number of songs portray the trauma of a father who is unable to be with his children and watch them grow up or—even worse—knows they are being raised by another man. The heartbreak of Hank Williams' "My Son Calls Another Man Daddy" is reprised from another angle in "I Don't Call Him Daddy" (Reed Nielsen), recorded by both Kenny Rogers and Doug Supernaw. An estranged father is on the road and hasn't contacted his son in three weeks. He calls him up on the phone, asks how he is, and asks, "How's your momma now/And her new live-in friend?"

Her "live-in friend"! This contemporary living arrangement may be harder to deal with than an ex's remarriage. But the child tries to reassure his father, telling him not to worry, that he does not call him Daddy, that he can never take his father's place. The childish preoccupations (asking if he is going to get a present) are mingled with the pathos of a child affectionately trying to comfort his dad, even though he is not there to perform the role of father. That role is being performed by the "live-in," who "takes care of things." The song becomes a meditation on children as the true casualties of divorce. The boy's precocious understanding does not take away the fact that the boy is crying.

In Toby Keith's "Who's That Man?" an ex-husband drives around his old neighborhood. He used to drive home this way every day. He notices that the county has finally fixed the road. He drives by his old home and sees, from a distance, his children, his ex-wife, and her new husband. The very ordinariness of the life he sees around him, a life that is no longer his, adds to the heartbreak. He decides not to stop. They are not expecting him. It might cause a scene. Although the kids had gone through rough times, he reflects, slipping into postdivorce banality, "I hear they adjusted well." The song's understatement and restrained emotion only add to the tension. This is not the way it is supposed to be.

An ex-husband's expressions of regret sometimes become musings on whether his wife might take him back. These musings often come close to the Christian definition of repentance and desire for forgiveness. This attitude is displayed in one of the most beautiful tunes in country music, "Make the World Go Away" (Hank Cochran), performed by Eddie Arnold:

> Do you remember when you loved me,
> Before the world took me astray?
> If you do, then forgive me,
> And make the world go away.

The singer says that he's "sorry if I hurt you" and promises to "make it up day by day." But, of course, the world doesn't go away, at least not for long.

8

Country Music's Moral Tradition

DRINKIN', CHEATIN', AND FAMILY VALUES

One of the most moving songs of repentance is by Billy Joe Shaver—the songwriter whose tunes about the rough and rowdy life, written for Waylon Jennings, helped define the Outlaw movement in country music. Shaver—who lived the life that he was writing music about—later turned to Jesus. His religious songs bring the gospel into the context of gritty, soul-wrenching country angst. In "If I Give My Soul," he writes of his need for forgiveness, not only from Jesus but from the woman he left. Here again is the motif of the fool. The sin that is weighing on him has to do with his alcoholism and how he has treated his wife and son. His wife was gentle and kind, and their son grew up to be a man. The singer recounts how he had a steady job until he started drinking, turning instead to music and falling in with the devil.

The chorus expresses the hope, nearly too plaintive for words, that perhaps his reconciliation with the Lord might mean reconciliation with his family. If he gives his soul to Jesus, "will he stop my hands from shaking?" Will his son love him again? "If I give my soul to Jesus, will she take me back again?" As this song suggests, the notorious country music motifs of drinking and cheating are nearly always set within the larger theme of heartbreak caused by a broken marriage bond.

Drinkin' Songs

Some drinking songs, to be sure, are exuberant celebrations of "The Honky Tonk Attitude"—in the words of a Joe Diffie title (with Lee Bogan). David Lee Murphy's "Party Crowd" is about a honky-tonk paradise, thick with smoke and loud with laughter, with dancing in one corner and fighting in another. The fighting is just as much a part of the soothing atmosphere as the dancing. The rollicking chorus expresses a good-time apathy (with the "juke box jumpin' like it just don't care"), a desire to find a party crowd that just wants to have fun. Yet the verse is the familiar country angst. When she told him good-bye, both of their hearts were breaking. That is why he came to the honky-tonk: "misery looking for some company."

Getting drunk at the honky-tonk is not recreation; it's escape. Drinking is often portrayed as escape from one's job, from a week of hard, backbreaking labor (as in Brooks and Dunn's "Hard Working Man," Sammy Kershaw's "Honky Tonk America," and innumerable songs about blowing one's paycheck on Saturday night). But usually, country drinking songs—especially the slow ones—depict escape from the heartbreak of lost love, another way of dealing with loneliness.

This is the sentiment in Willie Nelson's "Whiskey River" (Johnny Bush, Paul Stroud): "Whiskey River take my mind/ Don't let her mem'ry torture me." And it is the sentiment in Brooks and Dunn's "Neon Moon" (Ronnie Dunn), with its lovely melancholy melody: "When the sun goes down on my side of town,/That lonesome feeling comes to my door/And it turns my world blue." He goes to a run-down bar on the other side of the tracks and gets a table for two, where he sits by himself and thinks about losing her. "I spend most every night beneath the lights of a neon moon."

But these songs bear testimony that numbing the mind cannot really anesthetize the pain. This is stated plainly in "The Whiskey Ain't Workin'," a duet from Travis Tritt and Marty Stuart (Marty Stuart, Ronny Scaife): "When the thought of you came crashin' through, I'd have one more/But now the whiskey ain't workin' anymore." Not that this necessarily stops him from trying.

Alcoholism has been a plague among country artists. It killed Hank Williams—combined with his drug addiction. George Jones was in a drunken haze for a good part of his career, leading him to miss performances and earning him the ignominious title of "No-Show Jones." Johnny Cash fought the bottle, as did others too numerous to mention.

Even Ira Louvin—so talented at writing songs denouncing sin, extolling conservative theology, and denouncing the evils of the bottle—was an alcoholic, a mean drunk who would smash his mandolin when it was out of tune, get into fights (including a notorious encounter with Elvis Presley), and kick out the television screen when he caught his son watching *American Bandstand*.[1] When Louvin sang his antialcohol songs, such as "The Kneeling Drunkard's Plea," listeners were spared from moralism or pietism by the realization that *he* was that kneeling drunkard.

Since most country music performers acknowledge traditional morality, even when—or especially when—they are violating it, their struggles with the bottle are portrayed as intense moral struggles. The devastating consequences on their marriages and family life heighten the guilt. Again, that loving bond is broken, and the result is a compound of guilt, despair, and drunken self-pity.

Recently, hit songs have come out of the struggle to break an addiction. These songs typically depict a virtuous wife with whom the alcoholic wants to reconcile and are full of religious imagery. Kenny Chesney's "That's Why I'm Here" (Shaye Smith, Mark Alan Springer) centers on an Alcoholics Anonymous meeting. The protagonist has stopped by his estranged wife's house one night to try to tell her what he has learned, but first he has to reassure her that he hasn't been drinking. He asks if she remembers how he had promised her to someday go to one of those meetings at the YMCA. Well, he did, and when they started talking about taking all those steps he nearly walked away. But then, he tells her, an old man got up and told his story: "It's the simple things in life"—your kids, your wife—"That you miss the most, when you lose control." The old man tells about losing everything he loves and the devil urging him to drink. The singer recognizes, in the old man's words, his own life. It is obvious that he too lost his family because of his drinking, that he misses his wife and kids and everything that he had thrown away. He asks his estranged wife if she would come with him when he stands up to give his own AA testimony.

Mark Chesnutt's "Thank God for Believers" (Mark Alan Springer, Roger Springer, Tim Johnson), is about a recovering alcoholic who has fallen off the wagon. As discussed in chapter 5, his wife's recourse to the Bible and prayer symbolize her belief in both God and her husband. It is this belief that has given her the strength not to give up on him. He is filled with gratitude for her faithfulness and steadfast love, despite everything he has put her through. She tells him not to give up, to keep fighting. "Sunday morning here beside her in the pew,/Through bloodshot eyes I try to see her point of view." In this song, the husband's struggle with the bottle is given a spiritual dimension. He thanks God for his wife, and at the end of the song, he is hung over, but in church with her.

Similarly, in Collin Raye's "Little Rock" (Tom Douglas), an estranged husband calls up his ex-wife. He says he hasn't had a drink in nineteen days—an exact count characteristic of an alcoholic trying very hard to stop drinking, taking it as AA recommends, one day at a time. He has moved to Little Rock, Arkansas, to get a new start and has a job selling VCRs at Wal-

Mart. He is going to church and begs his ex-wife to take him back. "Without you, baby, I'm not me."

The religious imagery in an alcoholic's song becomes especially poignant in T. Graham Brown's "Wine into Water" (with Bruce Burch, Ted Hewitt). Hitting rock bottom, the protagonist turns to prayer and asks God for a miracle that reverses what He did in the Bible. Now, at his lowest, on his knees he asks that God, who once turned water into wine, "help me turn the wine back into water." He talks about hurting the ones he loves and how he used to shake his fist at heaven. But "Now I'm beggin' for forgiveness and a miracle from you."

Cheatin' Songs

Even the negative content of country music songs tends, indirectly, to support traditional values. This is also true of the other controversial obsession of country music—the large number of songs about adultery; that is to say, cheating.

There are a few country songs that seem to celebrate adultery. Reba McIntire's "Little Rock" (Pat McManus, Quentin Powers) is a far cry from Collin Raye's song of the same name about alcoholism. The woman is "married to the good life," with a Mercedes, tennis club, and the ability to "buy all the finer things." "But all that don't mean nothing," she complains, "when you can't get a good night's loving."

This song may be a class-envy song, repeating the common motif of how rich people are not happy after all and how rich women—or women who marry for money—would be happier with a poor man. (This motif is found in old standards such as "Silver Threads and Golden Needles" [J. Rhodes, D. Reynolds] and in contemporary hits like John Michael Montgomery's "Cowboy Love" [Bill Douglas, Jeff Wood]; Garth Brooks' "Friends in Low Places" [Dewayne Blackwell, Bud Lee]; and Aaron Tippen's "That's As Close As I'll Get to Loving You.") Still, the woman in "Little Rock" is unusually cold-blooded in her contempt for marriage, as she sings—to a sprightly, upbeat melody—about slipping off her wedding ring with its diamond ("the little rock") for an unfaithful night on the town. In the words of the chorus: "Oh, little rock;/I think I'm going to have to slip you off./Take a chance tonight and untie the knot."

Such a character—the loose woman, the temptress—is not uncommon in country music, usually in songs from a woman worrying about someone stealing her man. (For example, Loretta Lynn's "You Ain't Woman Enough"; Lee Ann Womack's "The Fool" [Maria Cannon, Gene Ellsworth, Charlie Steff]; The Dixie Chicks' "Tonight, the Heartache's on Me" [Johnny Mac-Rae, Bob Morrison, Mary W. Francis].)

A similar song from a male point of view at least has undertones of guilt, with a somber, melancholy melody. Moe Bandy's "It's a Cheating Situation" (C. Putman, S. Throckmorton) is forthright about committing adultery, but there is not much enthusiasm about it: "It's a cheating situation/A stealing invitation/To take what's not really ours." He knows it's a cheap imitation, though. They are just "doing what we have to do/When there's no love at home."

The man knows what he is doing is wrong—it's "stealing" as well as cheating. His justification, as in the Reba McIntire song, is that there is no love at home. He does what he feels he has to do, but he knows that this affair is just a "cheap imitation" of what the relationship between a man and a woman should be. His girlfriend is apparently in the same situation. "Sweetheart," he tells her, "We both know/We'll take love where we find it./It's all we've got." But they both know the affair will go nowhere. "There's no use in pretending/There'll be a happy ending."

Waylon Jennings' "Broken Promise Land" (Wilburn S. Rice) is in the same vein. The sense of transgression is heightened by the Christian imagery, both of the title and the Gideon Bible on the dresser of the cheap hotel room, where a couple is having a sleazy, adulterous one-night stand.

Part of the sordidness of the scenario is the deception of the man's wife. He puts no blame on her; it isn't that his home life is without love. This is sheer, soulless lust. But it has become a pattern to him. It's a cheating *life* that is nothing new to him. He picks up the phone and calls his wife, saying that he has to work late. The adulterer hates himself for his cheating. He goes home to his wronged wife but finds a little surprise: A note on the dresser, the house key, and her wedding ring thrown on the floor. Now she is "heading for the broken promise land."

His wife saw through him. She knew. She takes off her wedding ring, and now she is headed for the broken promise land. "Tonight she's crossing over"—another painful biblical allusion to the Promised Land—but she is crossing over to "the cheating side." Both of them are headed not for the land of milk and honey but its opposite—the fallen world, where "lives are built on lies." The breaking of the wedding promises is not only adultery but—undoubtedly the ultimate destination—divorce.

Most cheatin' songs, though, are not about the perpetrators but about the victims. Loretta Lynn and Tammy Wynette sang songs about unfaithful husbands that were filled with both hurt and defiance. Conversely, wronged men in such songs sometimes turn violent, tormented by the thought that their wives have been unfaithful. Thus we have Porter Wagner's "Cold Hard Facts of Life" (Bill Anderson) about a man coming home early from a trip, bearing flowers and champagne, only to find his wife with another man, a surprise ending with a murder by knife. Then there is the black humor of Garth Brooks' "Papa Loved Mama" (with Kim Williams), a narrative about a truck driver running his rig into the motel room of his cheating wife, all told from the point of view of their little boy! ("Mama's in the graveyard, papa's in the pen.") Sometimes the songs project another kind of revenge: the woman paying back a cheating husband by doing the same thing to him. Jan Howard threatens "Your Good Girl's Gonna Go Bad" (Billy Sherrill, Glenn Sutton). In Brooks and Dunn's song on the subject, "She's Not the Cheatin' Kind" (Ronnie Dunn), a woman, furious with her cheating, lying husband, is provoked by his actions to do what she really does not want to do: cheat on *him*.

The usual mood of cheating songs, though, is simmering jealousy, suspicion, and bitterness. In Daryle Singletary's "I Let Her Lie" (T. Johnson), the husband knows the truth but lets the lies build and build. She says she's been out with friends, but "I let her lie." She swears that he's the only one, but he let her lie. He is in a state of his own self-deception and denial. They even had • **127** a reconciliation in which she cried and—notice the religious language—confessed her sins and promised not to cheat on him anymore. But this was a lie too, and he "let her lie." Finally, one morning he left her. "She was sound asleep in our double bed," but, with no word of good-bye, in a characteristic country music wordplay, he "let her lie."

The theme of denial is also evident in Toby Keith's "I Wish I Didn't Know Now (What I Didn't Know Then)." He never asks her where she is going or where she has been—he does not want to know. He never calls to check her stories. When he knows the truth—which he wishes he didn't—he realizes that he should leave her. But he doesn't want to. He would seize on any excuse to stay. "Please don't say you're sorry,/I might wait another day."

Ernest Tubb often wrote about the worry and the agony of a man being cheated on, but in his little story-songs, the love the husband still feels for his errant wife is usually undamaged. This is the gist of his trademark song, "Walking the Floor Over You": She has broken her wedding vows, left him, and he doesn't know why. But he still calls her dear. He still loves her, despite how she has treated him. He is still waiting for her. Not only that, he is praying. "I'm hoping and I'm praying as my heart breaks right in two./Walking the floor over you."

In another tune, "Two Wrongs Don't Make a Right," Tubb explicitly repudiates the pay-you-back-in-kind response to adultery: "Now, when I caught you cheatin', dear, I could have cheated, too. But two wrongs don't make a right." Instead, he will just be patient until she changes: "So, I'll just be patient, dear, until you see the light." An Ernest Tubb protagonist can sometimes be sarcastic, as in his famous "Thanks, Thanks a Lot" (Eddie Miller, Don Sessions), but his "jealous loving heart," in the words of another of his titles, shows arguably a more Christian response.

A rather remarkable song written and recorded by Randy Travis delves into the psychology of unfaithfulness. "The Reasons I Cheat" have to do not so much with sex as with living a failed, pathetic life. The reasons include: failure to get a promotion and being ignored by his boss; losing his hair; his children growing up. In short, "I'm getting older, my life's growing colder." When he meets "a willing young woman" in a "dimly lit tavern" who shows him affection, he turns to her "to help soothe my pride."

Also dealing with unfaithfulness is the whole subcategory of temptation songs. We have already discussed the rather prurient and blasphemous "Heaven's Just a Sin Away." Others are recent songs such as Trisha Yearwood's "Here Comes Temptation" (Kostas) and Marty Stuart's "Tempted," not to mention country music classics such as Hank Locklin's "Please Help Me I'm Falling" (Don Robertson, Hal Blair). Then there is the overblown religious imagery in Mindy McCready's "Ten Thousand Angels" (Steven Dale, Billy Henderson) in which a young woman who sees her old flame invokes 10,000 angels, which will probably not be enough to keep her from being led into temptation.

A more subtle use of a Christian subtext in a temptation song is David Houston's "Almost Persuaded" (Glenn Sutton, Billy Sherrill—also recorded by Lefty Frizzell and others). The opening stanza sets forth a vivid, sensual description, drawing the listener into what temptation feels like. Alone in a bar, a man meets a woman with ruby red lips and coal black hair, holding a drink. She has tempting eyes. She comes to his table. Holds his hand. He wants to kiss her. "And I was almost persuaded." They dance. She comes right out and propositions him. He looks into her eyes, where he sees reflected his wedding band. The exact posture that would make this physically possible is not clear. As in Keith Whitley's "On the Other Hand" (memorably performed also by Randy Travis), the wedding ring is an objective reminder of his commitment to his wife, which outweighs the passions of the moment. The sight of the wedding ring, reflected in the eyes of the temptress, reminds him of his marriage and the love he has for his wife. "And I was almost persuaded . . . But your sweet love made me stop and go home."

The reference to "strange lips" is a biblical allusion to the figure of the "strange woman" in the Book of Proverbs. Throughout Proverbs, verse after verse warns a young man about the temptation from this strange woman, that is, a woman he does **• 129** not know. "For the lips of a strange woman drop as an honey-comb, and her mouth is smoother than oil: But her end is bitter as wormwood, sharp as a two-edged sword" (Prov. 5:3–4). The young man to whom these teachings are addressed is enjoined instead to "rejoice with the wife of thy youth . . . and be thou rav-ished always with her love. And why wilt thou, my son, be rav-ished with a strange woman?" (Prov. 5:18–20). An additional Christian allusion in this song is its title, which is also the title of an old gospel song about being almost persuaded to follow the Lord. These multiple associations heighten the tension and give the whole song a spiritual resonance.

It is no wonder that songs growing out of a culture saturated with Christianity would treat sin—its allure, its inevitability, and its hellish consequences—in a frank way. The portrayal of sin, however, is in no way antinomian or even permissive; rather, it serves to reinforce the moral order.

Family Values

If country music often deals with the discord between a husband and a wife that can lead to divorce, its portrayal of the relationship between children and parents is almost always positive, even idealized. The country songs celebrat-ing mother—from Jimmie Rodgers through Hank Williams to the Confederate Railroad—have become part of the coun-try music stereotype. (The Confederate Railroad is the con-temporary redneck novelty band responsible for "Jesus and Mama" [Danny Mayo, James Dean Hicks] with the immortal lines "Jesus and mama always loved me, even when the devil took control.")

Country songs from a son's or daughter's point of view almost always venerate both mothers and fathers. Mothers, as we have seen, are always loving, devout, and understanding. Fathers tend to be strong, disciplining, and wise. We have seen this in Travis Tritt's "Where Corn Don't Grow." A touching tribute from a daughter's point of view is Holly Dunn's "Daddy's Hands." Con-versely, country songs from the parents' perspective tend to por-tray the love and responsibility they feel for their children.

There are very few exceptions to this positive portrayal of the relationship between children and parents. In Reba McIntire's "The Greatest Man I Never Knew" (Richard Leigh, Layng Martine Jr.), she complains about an emotionally distant father. More disturbing is Martina McBride's "Independence Day" (Gretchen Peters), which spins a tale about a daughter setting the house on fire to get rid of her abusive daddy (though he is abusive to his wife and not to the child). Such negative parental images, however, are extraordinarily rare, and they are nearly always modern, reflecting the contemporary pathologies of family life.

Much more representative of the country music tradition is "Mom and Dad's Waltz," written and performed by the great vocal stylist Lefty Frizzell. The song is inevitably sentimental, but it is sung with such sincerity and earnestness that it is strangely affecting:

> I'd walk for miles, cry or smile
> For my mama and daddy
> I want them, I want them to know
> Oh, I feel, my love is real
> For my mama and daddy
> I want them to know I love them so.

The lyrics read like a children's song, but it is a hulking, streetwise adult (called Lefty because of his left hook) who is calling his parents "mama and daddy" without a shred of self-consciousness and with utter honesty. He also prays for them. "And I pray every day for mom and pappy/and each night." His affection has a distinctly adult resonance:

> I'd fight in wars, do all chores
> For my mama and daddy
> I want them to live on, 'til they're called.
> I'd work and slave, and never rave
> To my mama and daddy
> Because I know I owe them my all.

In this stanza, what children do for their parents—the chores—is juxtaposed with what young men do for their parents—fight **· 131** in wars. The song was written in 1951, just a few years after World War II, while the Korean War was at its height.

Some of the strongest songs about the bonds between parents and children—and the agonizing struggles families sometimes have—are by Merle Haggard. The son of migrant workers who left Oklahoma for the labor camps of California during the Dust Bowl, Haggard knew the hardships that parents sometimes go through to raise their children. In "Mama Tried," he depicts a mother's worst nightmare, the child who rejects everything she has tried to teach him about how he should live his life. Perhaps thinking of his own misspent youth—and imprisonment in San Quentin for burglary—Haggard has the protagonist lay the blame squarely on himself. He was the one rebel child "from a family meek and mild." Even though he had been taught the right way, he kept turning to the bad. Now he is reaping the consequences:

> And I turned twenty-one in prison doing life without parole
> No one could steer me right but Mama tried, Mama tried.
> Mama tried to raise me better but her pleading I denied;
> That leaves only me to blame 'cause Mama tried.

Here a jailed criminal is taking responsibility for his own actions and defending his mother—perhaps against the sixties-style habit of blaming a person's upbringing for current misbehavior. Haggard hates that sort of thing, and knows better from his own experience.

Haggard is no bleeding-heart liberal, to say the least, but no one can write songs about genuine poverty the way he can. In "Hungry Eyes," Haggard describes, in autobiographical terms, a family's life in a labor camp: "My daddy raised a family there, with two hard working hands/And tried to feed my mama's hungry eyes." His mother's hunger for a better life was intensified by her social humiliation. Her faith was strong and his father dreamed of a better life, but "another class of people put us somewhere just below;/One more reason for my mama's hungry eyes." The father works hard, but they never get ahead. With country piety, he prays: "I remember daddy praying for a better way of life," but nothing changed. "Just a little loss of courage, as their age began to show/And more sadness in my mama's hungry eyes." Hardship just wears them down as they lose heart and get older and sadder.

In one of Haggard's most moving songs, "If We Make It through December," he describes the struggles of a poor family just trying to get by: "If we make it through December, ev'rything's gonna be alright I know." The husband and father is trying to be optimistic, to reassure his family. If we can just get through this month, everything will be fine. It will get warmer. We'll move. We'll be fine. He is a hardworking man, we learn, but he got laid off at the factory—at Christmastime no less. "Their timing's not the greatest in the world." He is torn up because he can't provide a good Christmas for his daughter. He "wanted Christmas to be right for Daddy's girl," who "don't understand why Daddy can't afford no Christmas here." But if they just make it through this one month, they can move to California. The irony is that we know, from his other songs about the labor camps, what awaits them there.

Haggard takes another tack with "The Farmer's Daughter," about a father whose daughter is getting married. Tonight there will be a wedding in the run-down country chapel. The farmer's eyes will be filled with tears because he has to "give my one possession to that city boy from town." Again we have the old country church, almost in ruins. There is also the familiar tension between the country and the city, though the farmer is cutting the boy some slack for his long hair. "His hair is a little longer than we're used to," but he guesses he should say something good about his future son-in-law, who won his daughter. As the song goes on, we learn that the farmer is a single father. His wife left eight years ago, making him a victim of a broken marriage. "It was hard to be a Dad and Mama too," he says, but "love was all my baby ever knew." As for this city boy with long hair,

> He could be the richest man in seven counties
> And not be good enough to take her hand.
> But he says he really loves the farmer's daughter,
> And I know the farmer's daughter loves the man.

To make his daughter happy, he is willing to stand aside.

In Haggard's songs, fathers and mothers are poor but digni-fied; the songs, with their haunting melodies, are both emo-tional and restrained, melancholy but life-affirming. In the same way, country music, taken as a whole, faces honestly the grim-ness, the heartache, and the weakness that human flesh is heir to, treating it all in an utterly authentic way. But when all is said and done, we are left with family values, values that are hard-won and grounded in a transcendent order beyond the self.

9

The Country Artist

HANK WILLIAMS VERSUS LUKE THE DRIFTER

Hank Williams is arguably the most important performer in all of country music. Emerging at precisely the midpoint of the twentieth century, he wrote and performed nearly every kind of country song—rollicking honky-tonk tunes and melancholy cheatin' songs, songs about love and divorce, mothers and children, drinking and adultery, moralism and sentimentality, death, despair, and above all, loneliness. He also wrote about Jesus and salvation and eternal life. Hank Williams displayed the very elements of sin and grace—both in the range of his music and the battle within his heart.

Like many Southern boys who eventually became country music performers, Hank

Williams had a strong dose of the Baptist church in his background.

Roger Williams, in his 1980 biography *Sing a Sad Song,* notes some early church-based influences in Hank's life:

> Hank's musical experience . . . started at the age of three. He sat on the bench with his mother when she played the organ at the Mt. Olive Baptist church, next door to their double pen home. Whether from this experience or not, he developed a love for and understanding of the old four-square hymns. They greatly influenced the songs he later wrote, and some people think his hymns are the finest work he ever produced.[1]

Williams never let go of the piety he soaked up from his mother and his church.

Yet Hank was an alcoholic, a womanizer, a drug addict. He would record earnest gospel songs with his wife, Audrey, but their marriage was a battle zone and ended in a bitter divorce. Hank would sometimes get so drunk he couldn't get on stage. And then, after supposedly being kicked by a horse, he got addicted to pain pills, which emaciated his body and dulled his mind. But he wrote songs like "I Saw the Light." He died in the backseat of his Cadillac from drug and alcohol poisoning. He was twenty-nine.

His biographer quotes a songwriter friend who tells about how Hank and Red Foley (author of such classic country gospel songs as "Peace in the Valley") would get together in a drugstore booth between sets at the Grand Ole Opry. They "discussed nothing but religion," the songwriter recalled. "Hank had some pretty deep thoughts on it, and so did Foley, though both of them drank like fish. I remember Hank saying that he knew what he was doing—drinking and what not—wasn't in keeping with his religious beliefs but that he believed them just the same."[2]

This is not hypocrisy, but *psychomachia,* the spiritual conflict between the flesh and the spirit, sin and grace. A similar conflict can be seen in other country artists and in country music as a whole.

Though he would mix his wild songs with his religious ones, Hank eventually went so far as to adopt another persona, Luke the Drifter, to record the religious and moral and gentle songs he most wanted to express. It is hard to know which side prevailed in Hank's short and troubled life, but though he hardly lived the victorious Christian life, he seems to have been a self-confessed desperate sinner whose only hope was in Christ's unmerited grace.

Sacred Songs and Early Recordings

Hiram King Williams was born in 1923 in small-town, rural Alabama. His mother was a church organist and taught him to love gospel music and hymns. His father, a victim of a poison gas attack in World War I, had to stop working because of poor health, whereupon seven-year-old Hank went to the streets to help support his family by selling peanuts and shoeshines. Here he met a black street singer named Rufus "Tee Tot" Payne who taught him about music. His mother gave him a $3.50 guitar when he was eleven. By the age of fourteen he had his own band, and before long he was playing for dances and medicine shows. Eventually a radio gig on a Montgomery station led to a bigger audience and ultimately to his recording career.

Williams' first professional recording session took place during December 1946 in Nashville—a mere six years before he would be found dead in the backseat of his Cadillac. At that time in the industry, each recording session was usually scheduled for three hours of studio time. Four usable songs were expected to be produced, which were subsequently released by the record company on two singles. Of the four songs he recorded, three of them were overtly, if not stridently, religious: "When God Comes and Gathers His Jewels," "(Can't You Hear the Precious Savior) Calling You," and "Wealth Won't Save Your Soul." The other song, "Never Again," was about love gone wrong.

The pattern was set for his subsequent career. From his first to his final session, Williams never changed his style. Even on his first recordings, all of the elements were firmly in place that •**137** would soon make him a star—his unmistakable voice, the straightforward delivery, the simple and pure country backing, and the quality of the songs themselves. Not only did the songs work musically, they had a sense of authenticity about them, presenting the joys and pains of life and relationships—whether with a woman or with God—in an utterly honest and convincing way. Williams wrote all four of the selections he recorded at his initial studio experience. This is not surprising, considering that producer Fred Rose—who discovered Williams—had originally hired Hank for his songwriting abilities. But with three-quarters of this original material being overtly religious in tone, it shows where Hank's interests and priorities in life and in music were at the time.

Hank's second session (held in February 1947) lacked the religious songs. As he struggled to begin his career in earnest, he recorded his hit "Honky Tonkin'," "My Love for You (Has Turned to Hate)", "I Don't Care" (two love-gone-wrong songs), and "Pan American" (a train song).

His third session (in April 1947) featured the novelty song "Move It on Over," about being in the doghouse, and two other secular tunes. But it also included "I Saw the Light." Although closely based on an earlier song and unsuccessful when first released, "I Saw the Light" became one of Hank Williams' best-known songs of faith.

Unlike some country music acts who began their recording careers in the late 1940s and early 1950s, Hank Williams had a great deal of freedom as to what he recorded and was not restricted by genre. Of course, producer Fred Rose was quick to tell Williams which songs he found appropriate to Hank's style and which ones seemed wrong. But Williams was fortunate in that he was never contractually obligated to record only a certain style of music. Such restrictions were common at the time, and often a performer who cut gospel records was not allowed to release secular songs and vice versa. That Williams was unfettered by subject matter is evident in these early sessions, as Hank shows impressive versatility with both secular and sacred numbers.

Though a new performer offering a fresh sound, part of Williams' appeal—if such a thing can be quantified—was that his sound harked back a generation, echoing a relatively distant time and place. His songs sounded different in many ways from the country music records being made and played on the radio in the late 1940s. As Colin Escott reminds us, when Hank Williams was beginning his recording career, Merle Travis' "Divorce Me C.O.D." was high on the charts, and novelty songs by Hank Thompson were beginning to get regular radio exposure.[3] Only twenty years after the Bristol Sessions, the evangelical nature of many of those recordings was a distant memory to most country music fans. The songs of Jimmie Rodgers were likewise forgotten by many and had even become unavailable—deleted from RCA Victor's catalog and from the minds of many of the country music fans of 1949.

Hank Williams rekindled the excitement found in both sacred and secular music for his audience. He reminded the country audience of the power of country gospel music, as well as the good times of the cavalier honky-tonker, all the while remaining true to his own fresh sound. Hank Williams single-handedly revitalized interest in traditional country music for many fans. In Williams' songs are the deep religious fervor and sincerity of the Bristol recordings at their best, as well as the light-hearted raciness of a Jimmie Rodgers tune. What he added to these traditions—and what perhaps brought them together—was a sense of individual, personal suffering that enriched and validated both kinds of music.

Certainly Hank Williams did not exist in a country music vacuum. Ernest Tubb was hugely popular, an advocate for Rodgers, and a tireless crusader for country music. Eddy Arnold, Hank Thompson, Tex Williams, and Red Foley were all having successful country music careers at the end of the 1940s. But Hank's backwoods sound connected with the audience immediately, on a different level than all other performers of his time. It wasn't that other performers lacked sincerity, but Hank Williams' music seemed to be written for and, more importantly, about the individual listener. • **139**

Williams once said that he could never sing a nonsense song like "Mares Eat Oats" or "Ragmop." Based on his protectiveness over his material, it seems that the songs he chose to record had great meaning for him, even when cast from the perspective of another person. He appeared unwilling, if not actually unable, to belittle the music or its themes—a depth of sincerity that arguably came through in his music. In one famous example, Hank pointedly refused a chance to appear on Milton Berle's network television program (a potentially huge opportunity for a musician to gain national exposure). Williams refused the offer because he was angry that, while acting as emcee some months earlier at a large stage show, Berle had used a hillbilly skit to mock Williams' performance. Hank was sincere about everything he did, and his music was to be taken seriously. He meant everything he sang.

His Cheatin' Heart

Even Hank's lighthearted, humorous songs usually have failure or rejection or something deeply serious built into them. In "Honky Tonk Blues"—the song that brought down the house at the Grand Ole Opry and launched him into a national career—a farmboy tells his "pa I'm goin' steppin' out" and goes to the honky-tonks in the big city. While he likes the dancing and the barhopping, ultimately he finds city life depressing and decides to "scat right back to my pappy's farm." This is the familiar country music motif of the evils of the city and the virtues of the country. While treated in a funny, self-deprecating way, the insight that the honky-tonk life brings not just pleasure but the blues is a serious moral lesson (another one that Hank knew but did not live by). "Move It on Over," which literalizes the cliché about being in the doghouse, is a comical treatment of marital discord. "Nobody's Lonesome for Me" is brilliantly witty, but it is also about the yearning to be loved. His clever song about bad luck has the chilling title "I'll Never Get out of This World Alive."

Hank has some beautiful love songs ("The Alabama Waltz"), but most of them are about love unrequited or betrayed. A common theme in these songs is a man who still loves his ex-wife, even though she is now married to someone else ("Wedding Bells"; "I Can't Help It [If I'm Still in Love with You]").

The heartbreak in Hank's songs is often due to the family being all askew, with the protagonist's place in the family structure being taken by someone else—as in what has been called the saddest title in country music, "My Son Calls Another Man Daddy." It should be emphasized that these songs are not necessarily autobiographical. In this latter song, for example, a man's wife has remarried and the child has forgotten his father because he is in prison. There is no clear order or progression in the Williams canon that could align any of these songs with either his spiritual journey or the problems in his own marriage—actually, he and Audrey did not get a divorce until shortly before his death. Country songs, as is often said, tell stories; they are fiction. Still, like other fiction, they reflect their author's sensibility.

"Cold, Cold Heart" is a remarkable treatment of mistrust and the frustration that comes from failed communication. In the story set up by the protagonist, an earlier relationship has hurt the woman, making her mistrustful and spoiling her relationship with him. This causes the couple to fight. In their anger, they say unkind words, words that bring tears. The protagonist loves her and hates to see her hurt, but he is frustrated at how cold she is to him and how he just cannot get through to her. The more he cares for her, the farther they drift apart. The singer laments, "Why can't I free your doubtful mind and melt your cold, cold heart?"

Other songs are in far less understanding moods: The ultimatum in "You're Gonna Change (or I'm Gonna Leave)," the bitter and hurt accusation of "Your Cheatin' Heart," the weariness of all the grief in "Weary Blues (from Waitin')," and the emotional backlash of just giving up in "My Love for You (Has Turned to Hate)"—another candidate for bleakest song title.

Hank Williams is the poet laureate of loneliness. It is in describing the aftermath of a broken relationship and the sense of empty isolation, made more intense by the memory of the lost love, that his lyrics are most compelling. These songs are striking for, among other things, their vivid imagery that evokes ·**141** a mood. In "Alone and Forsaken" (another candidate), the life and death of a couple's love is described by the life and death embodied in the seasons. They met in the spring when the blossoms, the pastures, and the meadows were all coming to life. But in the autumn, her love, like the leaves, withered and died. The man's wife has been unfaithful and has left him. In the winter, the earlier images of springtime life are taken up again, but now the flowers and grass are dead. The birds have gone silent, except for a whippoorwill crying in the darkness.

That whippoorwill, with its lonesome cry, would become a recurrent character in Hank's most famous songs. The last stanza includes other images of nature that convey the lonely mood—the sky is getting ever darker; a hound is baying in the distance. Significantly, the refrain of this song, which portrays possibly the rock bottom of human emotions, includes a desperate appeal to God: "Alone and forsaken by fate and by man/Oh, Lord, if You hear me please hold to my hand/Oh, please understand."

The conventional phrase is "forsaken by God and by man," but Hank Williams would never say that. He is forsaken by fate. The refrain is actually a prayer asking God to "hold to my hand," showing a relationship that is stronger and more reliable than human love. Above all, it is a prayer for God to "please understand."

Inarguably his greatest lyrical achievement, "I'm So Lonesome I Could Cry," nearly the whole song consists of what T. S. Eliot called "objective correlatives" to the emotion of loneliness. Here again is the cry of the whippoorwill. There is the sound of a train at midnight. There is the sense of time slowing down, as it does in moods of great depression. There is the odd figure of another bird, a robin who is weeping as the leaves fall. And finally, there is the strangely evocative image of a falling star, lighting up the sky in total silence. "And as I wonder where you are/I'm so lonesome I could cry." Only in the next to the last line do we learn the occasion of his loneliness, which seems to be echoed throughout the cosmos.

In "May You Never Be Alone," the poetry is not nearly as good, but it develops the same themes. Here is that bird again, perhaps with an explanation of its connotation in the other songs: as in Walt Whitman's "Out of the Cradle, Endlessly Rocking," the bird is calling into the darkness for its lost mate. The song goes on to rehearse a sad little narrative of love betrayed, and then, like "Alone and Forsaken," brings Christianity into the picture. God's Word, the Bible, says that every wrong must be paid for. But the song ends with a prayer that the Lord set him free, plus a prayer for the woman who has hurt him: "May you never be alone like me." The invocation of the Bible is vindictive, but it at least rings more true than the repeated wish in the refrain that the woman will never be as lonely as she has made him. But again, in this condition of emotional desolation it is up to the Lord to set him free.

"I'm So Tired of It All" expresses what can be described only as total, abject despair. All of his life, the singer confesses, he has been lonesome. He keeps missing happiness. All his dreams have died, casualties of broken promises. "In life and love, I've been a failure," he concludes. "And now I'm so tired of it all."

This is not just self-pity, it is self-contempt. Here the blame is not thrown on a woman who has mistreated the protagonist. The broken vows and promises are in the context of *his* failure. This is no mere lament for a love gone wrong. He has failed at love *and* he has failed at life. Lonesomeness is the way he is describing "all my life." Now he is tired of it all, the weary blues, willing to just give up. The mood would be suicidal except that, once again, God enters into the picture. He reflects that this life is transient, and death will come soon. Though he grouses that "no one will miss me" after he is dead, there is another world. He prays he will find the contentment that has always eluded him—which would have to involve forgiveness for his failures and love for his loneliness—a state that can never be fully known on earth, but that is promised "up there" in heaven.

The song would seem to be a late song, a despondent, world-weary assessment of a wasted life. But actually, it was written in 1947, at the very beginning of his career, which suggests that the complex emotional conflict between despair and faith may apply in all of the songs and all of his life to come.

The Gospel Songs

Hank Williams clearly understood himself to be a sinner in need of grace and forgiveness. This gives his gospel songs a sense of authenticity. What he has to say in these songs seems as real and persuasive as in his heartbreak songs. These are not just pious set pieces; rather, they address the issues raised in his other songs, and they address the failures in his own life. He is not presenting himself in his religious songs as a spiritual role model for listeners to follow. Some gospel singers tend to give us the sense that we are looking at a façade, a consciously crafted and well-rehearsed pious persona. Hank's gospel songs do not give that impression at all; they are sung with the same engagement and sincerity that is evident in all of his other songs. When Hank is preaching, he is preaching to himself.

In "Lost Highway" (Leon Payne), he sings with great conviction about being lost. The song is an antipilgrimage song, a symbolic journey on a road to the wrong destination. The singer describes himself as "a rollin' stone all alone and lost." His being alone is described as a moral fault, part of his "life of sin." The protagonist's downfall, according to the song, was due to cards, wine—the conventional vices of fundamentalist piety—but also the lies of a woman. Just as getting saved is often described as a single moment of conversion, the same is true here of getting lost. In this compressed story-song, the trip down the lost highway begins on the day he met the woman. At the time he was an ordinary young man, but "now I'm lost, too late to pray. Lord I paid the cost, on the lost highway." Too late to pray? This lost soul is despairing even of the possibility of salvation.

As discussed earlier, train songs had become a tradition in country music. But Hank Williams sings about "The Devil's Train" (C. Carlisle, M. Foree). The devil's train is beautiful and tempting. But those riding this train are hurtling out of control to eternal misery.

This is like Casey Jones' runaway train. It takes God to stop it. "Oh, Lord, please stop that devil's train/Before it is too late."

144 •

With this intervention, the devil's train gives way to the glory train and its free ride to heaven.

Compare this to other gospel train songs, with their belabored symbolism of Jesus being the engineer and the necessity of buying a ticket, all in the jovial atmosphere of a family vacation. Here the harrowing bondage of sin is emphasized, which in turn accentuates the gospel where—because of God's action—salvation is free.

Most of Hank Williams' religious songs are written in the style and form of church music. That is, they consist of regular stanzas suitable for group singing, as opposed to solo performances. Hymns are not usually highly personal effusions; rather, they set forth universal Christian truths applicable to everyone. Above all, hymns are collective performances, an occasion for Christians to join together in the communal expression of their faith. Many of Hank's religious songs are like hymns, simply setting forth biblical images (such as depictions of Christ on the cross or descriptions of heaven) or offering various gospel-style exhortations in a generally affecting way. To be sure, Hank was recording these songs for people to listen to on their phonographs, rather than to sing as a group in church. Still, even when the song is about a personal religious experience—such as "I Saw the Light"—it is usually possible to sing it together with other people, in a way that is not true of his nonreligious songs.

In fact, many of his religious songs are recorded with other singers joining in, usually in the same harmonies commonly used in church. Some are duets with his wife, Audrey. "These were duets only in the technical sense," observes Hank Davis. "Often they seem to be extensions of the couple's marital discord, as Miss Audrey fought Hank for dominance on every note."[4] Audrey had singing ambitions of her own, and Hank used his influence to promote her career. But their voices do not blend together, to say the least. In fact, it sounds like Audrey was trying to sing louder than her husband, as if she was competing with him. Those who know of their tempestuous relationship can almost hear the tension between them in these seemingly pious duets.

The effect, though, is to give the songs a flawed, human context that throws their redemptive message in higher relief.

Hank Williams' religious songs address other human beings and, being forms of exhortation or evangelism, are technically gospel songs as opposed to hymns. Ironically, as we have seen, some of his heartbreak songs do include prayers and are addressed to God. But his gospel numbers are generally addressed to a "you." He is trying, in some way, to evangelize the listener—and perhaps himself.

"Can't you hear the Blessed Savior calling you?" he asks in "Calling You." "When you've strayed from the fold," when your soul is troubled and burdened, when you have no friends, can't you hear Jesus calling? It is almost as if the troubles themselves are part of God's calling.

Whereas some religious songs use the promise of a happy life as bait, Williams uses not only troubles but death as reasons to turn to the Lord. Several songs are in the ancient meditative tradition of the *memento mori:* Remember that you are going to die. "The Angel of Death" is characteristically vivid. The song begins by involving the Scriptures, which warn us of the inevitability of death. The song goes on to describe what it is to die: the lights grow dim, your loved ones gather around weeping. "Can you face them" he asks, "and say with your dying breath/That you're ready to meet the Angel of Death?" This song is another exhortation in the form of a question: "Can you . . . ?"

More uncomfortable questions are raised in "A Home in Heaven," a duet with Audrey. People are building nice houses—but "where will you live after death?" You need to be "building a home in Heaven." And you need to get it finished soon, because death is lingering.

Another use of domestic imagery for a spiritual end is "A House of Gold," which is, in effect, another ancient meditative form, the *contemptus mundi*—a reflection on the transience and worthlessness of the things of this world in light of eternity. In this life, the song says, people will do anything for wealth—including steal, cheat, and lie. But the fires of judgment day will melt all of the silver and gold. Then the song gets personal, shifting to "I": "I'd rather be in a deep dark grave," knowing that he was saved, than live in a house of gold "and deny my God and doom my soul."

The old tradition of the personal testimony is exemplified in Hank Williams' most famous religious song, "I Saw the Light." Before the appearance of Christ in this song, the images are all of darkness, night, blindness. With Jesus, the images are not only of light but of seeing. A deft use of a biblical reference brings all of the imagery together and expresses how salvation is due solely to the grace of God and the action of Christ: "Then like the blind man that God gave back his sight/Praise the Lord, I saw the light."

Some testimonies can become so self-absorbed that the work of Christ gets lost in the telling, but Hank's songs are generally Christocentric. "Jesus Remembered Me," he sang with Audrey. "I was all alone and drifting on a lonely sea of sin"—note the familiar themes of loneliness and "drifting" (his band being the "Drifting Cowboys"; his alter ego, Luke the Drifter)—but, repeating the imagery of light dispelling darkness, "Jesus remembered me." His song "Jesus Died for Me" is a vivid meditation on the cross (another classic meditative genre). Jesus was "tortured and slain" for him. "As He hung there all alone," bleeding and dying, "He never stopped praying for me." On the cross, Jesus is now the one who is "all alone." The poet laureate of loneliness sees Jesus as sharing his condition, as bearing his griefs, as sharing his loneliness.

One of Hank Williams' most exuberant songs is "I'm Gonna Sing," which looks ahead to leaving this sad world and entering the state of Glory. It is striking how Hank's songs about Christ repeat the language and call to mind the same moods of the heartbreak songs but end with resolution in the cross. "Sometimes I get so weary inside," he says, but "Then I recall how my Jesus died." This is presumably the same weariness he lamented in "Weary Blues" and "I'm So Tired of It All." But in this song, the despair reminds him of Christ, who shared his condition. The mood changes into anticipation of the joy of **·147** heaven, where he will "sing, sing, sing"—a fitting and personal offering from a musical genius.

Luke the Drifter

Such religious songs seem rather devout to be coming out of the mouth of a drunk, a drug addict, a bad husband. Hank wasn't particularly seeing the light in his later career. But though "I Saw the Light" was recorded in 1948, toward the beginning of his career, he continued to record Christian songs all the way to the end of his life. In a larger sense, though, all of his songs are religious. And, to be sure, all of his songs, whether about Jesus or Hank's own sin, are what the old evangelicals called "blood songs."

One could argue that the gospel testimony numbers were story-songs, just as all his songs were, that the genre demanded first-person narratives and therefore it cannot be assumed that Hank's religious songs reflected any personal piety. But it is hard to imagine these songs being written by someone who did not believe them, especially an artist known for his sincerity. He did not have to record these gospel numbers; they were not big sellers. The only reason he recorded these songs has to have been because he wanted to, because they meant something to him. If being a Christian includes not only one who is a saint but also a sinner who desperately clings to Christ for forgiveness, then Hank Williams is a supreme Christian artist.

Another possible explanation for the contradiction between his faith and his life is that he was a hypocrite, professing certain beliefs while refusing to live up to them. This could be, except for the evidence of inner conflict that comes out again and again in his work. One of the oddest, and yet most telling, aspects of Hank's career is the way he adopted an alter ego, recording under the name of Luke the Drifter songs of gentleness, peace, moralism, and piety—in stark opposition to the often tormented songs he recorded under his own name.

As noted, Hank was free to record religious material, and he did so throughout his career, but his fame with his distinctive honky-tonk sound was a kind of trap. When a bar patron played a Hank Williams record on a jukebox, he had certain expectations. The market was demanding one kind of music. Of his eleven singles that were number one hits, his twenty-five that reached the Top 5, and his nine that made the Top 10, not one was a religious number. He apparently wanted the creative space to record some of the songs he really wanted to do, outside the shadow of being Hank Williams.

Hank recorded fourteen selections under the pseudonym of Luke the Drifter. These were undeniably different, not only in theme but in sound and tone, than the records made under the Hank Williams banner.

Any potential confusion over image is a risk for an artist. Hank had a set of songs he was so interested in recording that he was willing to take the risk, even though he probably knew the records would not be big sellers. While he occasionally performed one or two of these selections during personal appearances, he never appeared in public strictly as his alter ego or billed himself as Luke the Drifter. Not that anyone was fooled, since everyone knew who Luke the Drifter really was. It may well have been that Luke the Drifter was the singer's real, deep-down personality and that Hank was the alias. At the very least, Luke the Drifter was a way for Hank Williams to be more himself.

Williams did not make a big issue of his alter ego. In Nashville it was said that the identity of Luke the Drifter was the worst-kept secret in town. Hank didn't seem to care. On a surviving transcript of an early morning radio show, Hank introduces one (rare) Luke the Drifter performance as a song recorded by a good friend of his. Hank and the band chuckle, for they too were aware that it was well known who had recorded it. Hank never seemed to confuse his fans or the record buying public.

Adopting another identity is not unheard of in country music. Ferlin Husky had used an alter ego to record singles as his rube character Simon Crum, and the Statler Brothers recorded as Lester "Roadhog" Moran and the Cadillac Cowboys. But these were characters created for comedy. Hank Williams created his alter ego out of tragedy and presented in the words of one of his titles, "Pictures from Life's Other Side." This other side usu-   • **149** ally included tales of suffering caused by not following God's plan. Whereas Hank Williams' usual tales of woe were presented from the inside, from the viewpoint of a person struggling or suffering or sinning, the Luke songs presented them from a distance. The tone is not quite moralistic in the sense of being indignant or self-righteous; rather, the tone is sympathetic but sad, exhorting the listener to moral behavior through the contemplation of these cautionary tales. The character of Luke the Drifter comes across as an avuncular, wise old man (though Hank himself was only in his twenties).

The first set of the Luke the Drifter singles, "Beyond the Sunset" and "The Funeral," were among the most powerful religious statements Williams would make. Not surprisingly, neither side made *Billboard Magazine*'s country music charts. But in spite of tepid sales (compared with his numerous large hits), Williams had a certain pride about the Luke material. By 1950, when he started recording as Luke the Drifter, Hank's career was going very well, having delivered eight Top 10 singles for his record company, resulting in huge sales and profits for the label. He therefore had a great deal of leverage, and in the initial Luke the Drifter session he demonstrated this—not only by recording numbers that would obviously not become radio and jukebox hits but by recording two numbers that had copyrights not owned by his company. He hadn't written them himself, and normally at this time record labels would only release songs that they owned. "Beyond the Sunset" was an old gospel hymn by Blanche and Virgil Brock, with music by A. Rowswell. Wrapped around a single verse of the hymn is a long narrative, the poem "Should You Go First," written by Pittsburgh baseball announcer Albert Roswell. According to country music historian Bob Pinson, hymn and poem were welded together by Chickie Williams.

"The Funeral" was an old anonymous poem in the public domain, to which Fred Rose had penned some background music. Hank clearly had a strong desire to record these specific songs, using his clout to bend the rules so that he could deliver their strong messages about faith, belief, and following God's edict of patient waiting.

One of the characteristics of the Luke the Drifter recordings was their use of recitation. When recitations are mixed with singing, the format is usually a sung verse followed by the spoken recitation, and then another singing section. The form of "Beyond the Sunset" is somewhat unusual. Hank inverts this, with a long recitation at both the beginning and the end, placing the emphasis on the spoken sections.

The recitation in "Beyond the Sunset" is a man telling his wife that if she dies first, he will "live in memory's garden" until he can join her. The narrative continues its focus on parallels between memory and nature, with different flowers and seasons calling up different memories of her. The sung section has almost nothing to do with the recitation. It is a lovely stanza from the old gospel song evoking heaven as a new morning, after the sunset of death. Again we see Williams' fondness for the imagery of darkness being overcome by light:

> Beyond the sunset, oh blissful morning
> When with our Savior, Heaven is begun.
> Earth's toiling ended, oh glorious dawning
> Beyond the sunset when day is done.

It then reverts to being a memory song, how the man will remember his wife and follow her to heaven. He comforts himself with the assurance that "memory is one gift of God that death cannot destroy."

Unlike any of his other recordings, "The Funeral" is purely narrative, accompanied only by a steel guitar and a mournful Hammond organ. Probably Hank Williams' starkest work, it is a piece full of sorrow, raising unanswerable questions concerning the death of a child. Although Bob Pinson has traced the origins of this recitation to the late nineteenth century, Hank Williams makes it his own, as he did with most everything he touched as a country artist.

At the beginning of the piece Williams (as Luke) sets the scene of a rural church funeral for a black child. Much of the selection is delivered in character narrative, with Williams assuming the role of the African-American preacher who is conducting the service. Through this speaker, we hear reflections on faith, religion, God, and death. The preacher admonishes the grieving parents not to be sad for this little mound of clay; he is with his "sho-nuff father" in heaven. Lines such as these could be ludicrous—or racist—in the wrong hands, but Hank Williams is able to deliver them unflinchingly, making the listener believe and ponder each word—because Hank believes the messages being given. Why otherwise would a performer at the top of his career as a honky-tonk singer, chief representative of a genre strongly associated with themes of infidelity and alcohol, record this movingly sad portrait? Recall his aversion to nonsense lyrics; he could not sing a song that was meaningless to him.

The preacher's admonishment to "not go criticizin' the one what knows the best" rings strongest near the end, along with an angel's assurance to the child in heaven concerning his parents, that "if only they be faithful they soon be comin' 'long to join him." The preacher reminds the parents at the service that as God "has given us many comforts, He's got the right to take away." The preacher further encourages the parents to think of the little boy as having been on loan to them only for a while to bring them joy.

Both "The Funeral" and "Beyond the Sunset" stress the glorious reunion of loved ones in heaven as the basis for hope in present suffering. In the meantime, those left behind must wait patiently, with their memories, passing through this world in faith.

This initial session—a session aimed at recording four songs to be released as two two-sided singles—produced two additional Luke the Drifter recordings, "Too Many Parties and Too Many Pals" and "Everything's OK." The first is a portrait of a girl corrupted by society. The girl who has gone wrong should not be judged harshly. She got involved with the wrong friends and started going to too many parties, which led to her moral downfall. While heartfelt, it pales in comparison to the impact delivered by both "Beyond the Sunset" and "The Funeral." What is most striking is the excruciating irony in Luke primly denouncing the venues and the lifestyles that were Hank's everyday existence. This song displays once again the conflict between Hank and Luke, and it is clear that Luke, as his moral center, has his greater sympathy.

The other selection, "Everything's Okay," lives up to its name of inspired optimism. Another character narrator, an Uncle Bill, recounts the woes of farm life, but always concludes his lament with the tag line, "but we're still a-livin' so everything's OK." The catalog of ills, delivered with easygoing optimism, becomes humorous as they get worse and worse. Everybody in the family is sick. The hogs have all died of the cholera. The porch and the fence have fallen down. Uncle Bill can't pay the mortgage. His mother-in-law has moved in. There is no food. The crops have failed. His wife just told him another baby is on the way. The bank turned him down for a loan, so they will probably lose the farm.

> But we're still a-livin' and we're prayin' for better days
> So after all, ever'thing's in purty good shape.

The tension between this catalog of one disaster after another and the notion that Uncle Bill still thinks "everything's OK" is humorously ironic. But there is genuine strength here: as long as they are alive, they are fine; they will not let lesser problems destroy their spirits. They deal with these problems as they come, with prayer. This is a comic version of the same theme found in "Beyond the Sunset" and "The Funeral"—overcoming suffering by patience and hope.

Hank Williams sporadically recorded as Luke the Drifter throughout his brief career. In addition to this January 1950 date, he again devoted specific recording sessions to Luke the Drifter numbers in August and December of 1950, and June and July of 1951, producing a total of fourteen tracks. There are other fine selections among the remaining ten numbers, including "Men with Broken Hearts," "Pictures from Life's Other Side," and "Be Careful of Stones You Throw." There is another novelty song in the vein of "Everything's OK," called "Just Waitin'," and even a unique political statement in "No, No Joe"—a mocking rejection of Joseph Stalin composed by Hank's producer, Fred Rose.

The most notable of the Luke recordings was the plaintive "Help Me Understand," an original composition by Williams. Hank uses his Luke the Drifter persona to articulate the pain • **153** of a young girl whose parents have recently divorced. The narrator, Luke, overhears the little girl praying. The mother tells the little girl that her daddy has gone away because he has brought shame on the family, implying that he had been unfaithful. The little girl is told "never no more to mention his name." The song makes a strong statement for "more honest lovin' in this wicked world," with pointed comments on the concepts of vanity, pride, and especially forgiveness. It is strongly antidivorce, which again puts Luke in direct conflict with Hank, not only in his songs but in his personal life.

This conflict is what gave all of Hank's songs their complexity and their authenticity. It is the conflict between sin and grace that, to one degree or another, constitutes the spiritual life of every Christian. More broadly, Hank Williams/Luke the Drifter embodied within himself the polarities and contradictions—and their occasional reconciliation—that characterize country music.

10

Contemporary Country Music

The state of country music in any given year is reflected in the annual Country Music Association awards. Roughly equivalent to the film world's Academy Awards, the CMA awards are given by members of the industry itself, as opposed to fans or critics. The Country Music Association not only looks after the interests of the record producers, studio musicians, technicians, disk jockeys, and artists, it is the steward of the Country Music Foundation, which operates the Country Music Hall of Fame Museum in Nashville and holds extensive recording and research archives. So respected is the Country Music Foundation as a center for cultural preservation that its director, William Ivey, was nominated by President Clinton and confirmed unanimously by Congress as the director of the National Endowment for the Arts.

The CMA Awards, like country music, have always had a ring of authenticity about them. As a television production, designed to highlight country music before a national audience, it tends to earn big ratings—since unlike the Oscars and the Emmys, the CMA makes a point of putting on a good show. But in 1999, not everything went according to script. The last award show of the twentieth century embodied what country music had become—a battleground between traditionalists and progressives, between the heirs of a folk culture and the products of pop commercialism.

The late nineties saw a decline in country music's market share, and many fans felt Nashville was in a creative malaise. And yet, a few performers not only became megastars, they broke out of the confines of country circles alone into the pop market, dominating every sales chart and getting massive airtime on noncountry radio stations. Garth Brooks passed Elvis Presley in record sales, putting him second in all-time sales only to the Beatles (on whom he was gaining). Shania Twain became the biggest-selling female country artist of all time, and one of the most successful in all of music, hitting it big even on MTV. Garth and Shania were not the usual country artists. They were relatively twang-free, contemporary in focus, and savvy about emulating the mass charisma and the high-energy stadium shows of rock stars.

The Dixie Chicks, on the other hand, achieved huge crossover success while still remaining part of the great country tradition, having honed their musicianship and paid their dues as a fringe-wearing cowgirl bluegrass group. They added a brash attitude, glamorous designer fashions, and rhythmic variations to traditional country themes and story-songs. Their songs about competition for a man ("There's Your Trouble" [Tia Sellers, Mark Selby]), leaving home ("Wide Open Spaces" [Susan Gibson]), and getting jilted ("Tonight, the Heartache's on Me" [Mary W. Francis, Johnny Macrae, Bob Morrison]), struck that

156 •

down-to-earth emotional chord for which country music is famous. Their music managed to be contemporary and original, while still sounding like traditional country songs. Their self-penned song about the emotional aftermath of a woman's divorce, "You Were Mine," applied country poignancy to the theme of contemporary family breakups. A woman questions what right her ex-husband had to leave her, offering two reasons why he should have stayed: "He's two and she's four and you know they adore you."

Such honesty in portraying children as the casualties of divorce had a resonance far beyond country fans. Yet the Dixie Chicks refused to tone down their twang or their fiddle. (Supposedly the music video channel VH–1 had offered to play their videos, if they would only drop the fiddle, which they indignantly refused to do.) Still, they were considered hip enough to get invited to participate in Lilith Fair, the all-woman traveling tour, featuring mostly feminist rock and rollers. The Dixie Chicks' albums *Wide Open Spaces* and *Fly* hit the top of the album charts and stayed there, month after month.

The prospect of such crossover success became the grail quest for lesser-known artists. More broadly, in trying to get the biggest market share, country radio stations began favoring songs that would appeal to the widest possible audience. As a result, much of country radio began sounding like rock and roll. And what didn't sound like rock and roll sounded like pop ballads. The various musical genres often became indistinguishable. In 1995, "I Can Love You Like That" (S. Diamond, J. Kimball, M. Derrywhich) was a number one hit for both John Michael Montgomery on the country charts and All-4-One on the pop charts.

In 1996, Leann Rimes, a fourteen-year-old musical prodigy, breathed life into traditional country with her rendition of "Blue," which begged comparison to Patsy Cline. The song, in fact, had been written by Bill Mack for Patsy before her death, and it found its way to this Texas child, who performed it with such maturity and virtuosity—with such phrasing and expressiveness and haunting beauty of tone—that traditionalists took heart. Here was a young talent—very young—who boded well • **157** for the future. This talented teenager continued to strike traditional chords, but to a certain extent, she began to be pulled in the pop direction by some of her handlers. In 1997, she was recruited to sing a song, "How Do I Live (without You?)" (D. Warren) for a Disney movie, but it was felt that the sultry lyrics were unsuitable coming out of a child so young, so Trisha Yearwood was brought on board instead. When both versions were released as singles, Trisha Yearwood's version won a Grammy for Best Female Country Vocal Performance. Leann Rime's version, on the other hand, was a smash hit, spending sixty-nine weeks on the charts, thirty-two of which were in the Top 10—not on the country charts but on the pop charts.

By 1999, listeners to country had become used to asking themselves, with song after song, "Now how is that country?"

The CMA had generally always been on the traditionalist side, but in 1999 the CMA Award nominations reflected the new commercial realities. Shania Twain, long a Nashville outsider unfairly scorned by the country music establishment, could no longer be ignored and was nominated for (and won) Performer of the Year. The Dixie Chicks also had many nominations (and won Vocal Group of the Year and Single of the Year). Instead of fighting the marriage of pop and country, the producers of the TV show decided to highlight it—and try to broaden country's sagging market share—by having country stars do duets with pop stars. Alabama would sing with 'N Sync. And the great Merle Haggard—the scourge of the sixties' counterculture, for whom "the hippies down in San Francisco" brought out "the fightin' side of me"—was paired with the neo–flower child waif, Jewel.

Throughout most of the decade, the still-living giants of country music—while being revered in word and welcomed on the Grand Ole Opry—were in exile from country radio and thus from major record sales. Though some of these artists were making the best music of their careers, they found themselves ignored by the music industry they had helped to found. Johnny Cash received the Grammy for Best Country Album of 1996 for his magnificent *Unchained,* a recording that expressed both the height of his musical artistry and his hard-won Christian piety.

But though it blew the critics away, won the respect of his peers, made even rock and rollers sit up and take notice—and won the Grammy—not a single track won airtime on country radio. When it won the award, his label took out a full-page ad in *Billboard*, showing a photo of Cash in his rough and rowdy days making an obscene gesture, with the caption directed to country radio. This ad seemed uncharacteristic of Cash, now a Christian—and as at the time he was hospitalized and incapacitated from a serious illness, it is unlikely that he had anything to do with placing the ad. But it nonetheless accurately reflected the bitterness with which country giants and their advocates were taking the disrespect they were feeling from their own industry.

In 1999, however, George Jones had a new song on the charts, and it was nominated for CMA's Song of the Year. The man in possession of what may be the most expressive voice in country music lived the life portrayed in his songs. He was married numerous times—including a stormy marriage with someone who could only be described as his female counterpart, Tammy Wynette, with whom he recorded some of the greatest duets in the history of country music. But no one could ever deny the power, poignancy, and sincerity of his voice ("He Stopped Loving Her Today," "The Grand Tour," "Tender Years," "She Thinks I Still Care"). Jones became an icon for fans of true country. When Alan Jackson, who is something of a standard bearer for traditionalists—but nevertheless has managed to score hit after popular hit—sang "Don't Rock the Jukebox," he stated clearly what he wanted instead of rock and roll: "I wanna hear George Jones!"

In 1998, Jones had published a mostly repentant autobiography, *I Lived to Tell It All*, which put him on the talk show circuit. This exposure combined with the death of his ex-wife Tammy Wynette, attracted new attention to his colorful career. He renounced his bad reputation as "No-Show Jones," hosted a TV show on TNN (consisting mostly of conversations with old-time greats), and started touring again. But then in 1999, the newspapers recorded what seemed to be the preordained end of George Jones. He had been in a car wreck, driving while •**159** drunk. After being close to death, however, Jones—ever the survivor—pulled through.

Soon after this incident, Jones released a song entitled "Choices" (Billy Yates, Mike Everett Curtis). Actually, it had been recorded before the wreck. And it was written for him by other songwriters. But the timing and the ironies, the autobiographical flavor, and the confessional way he sang it were startling. In the song, he soberly takes stock of his life and honestly and openly accepts responsibility for all of his bad choices. "I've had choices since the day that I was born." He leaves himself no excuses. He was taught the difference between right and wrong. If only, he says ruefully, he had listened.

At an early age, the song continues, he discovered that he liked drinking, and he never turned it down. He turned away all of his loved ones. He wishes he could go back. And he doesn't say it has gotten any better. But in the words of the refrain he is "living and dying, with the choices I made." This was vintage Jones—heartfelt, emotionally compelling, and sung like a grievous angel. It got on the radio. And it was nominated for Song of the Year.

The producers of the CMA television show were planning to have the nominees for the top awards perform at least some of their numbers. The focus, though, was clearly on the up-and-coming stars, especially those with broad crossover appeal. Shania Twain, beautiful and wearing one of her trademark sexy costumes, would do a big production number. The Dixie Chicks would be prominently featured. Other photogenic young stars would get some valuable exposure to a national audience. And then there would be those killer duets. Merle and Jewel! Both tradition and new country would be served, at the same time. Jewel fans and all the Lilith Fair devotees would see just how hip and respectable and relevant country music really is. As for George Jones, well, "Possum" (as he was known for his scrunched-up face and beady little eyes) could play a few bars of "Choices," but there really wouldn't be time for the whole song.

Jones refused to be patronized. If he couldn't play the whole song—his wrenching, personal confession of sin, nominated for Song of the Year, no less—he wasn't going to do it at all. He would boycott the whole phony show. He would become "No-Show Jones" once again, but this time out of his own personal dignity and artistic integrity.

The producers had no interest in backing down. If the old man didn't want to be on, that was his problem. The show went on, live, with its programmed glitz and glamour. There were a few miscues. The long-time host of the event, the affable, quick-witted Vince Gill, obviously did not like the material written for him. The teleprompter had him making some uncharacteristically vulgar jokes. He had to sing the theme from *The Brady Bunch* as the Wilkinsons walked up to the stage, needlessly insulting the family group that won accolades for "26 Cents," one of the most moving mother songs in years. But the TV producers must have thought the song was not hip enough, so they had to make fun of it. Gill had at first refused his part in this.

In the course of the awards show, Alan Jackson took his turn, giving a preview of his new single. The song, "Pop-a-Top" (Nat Stuckey) was an odd choice, a remake of an old performance by Jim Ed Brown. It had an old sound, harking back to the bygone days of country music. Its ostensible subject was popping the top of a beer can open, but could it have been one of those notorious country puns at work, a statement about "pop" music and how it is "atop" the traditional sounds he loves? As the band moved into the bridge, the key changed, the tune segued into another melody. Jackson was singing a different song: "I've had choices, since the day that I was born."

Mr. "Don't Rock the Jukebox" sang some Jones. Defiantly and against the script, he sang George Jones' song, in tribute to the man and to the stand he took. As the traditionalists in the crowd cheered, and the TV cameras tried to figure out what to do, Jackson quickly strode off the stage, not staying for the camera photo-op as planned. Flustered, the next two female presenters were caught somewhat agape when they said, "Oh, we're on. And now the winner of Male Vocalist of the Year will join us. Or we sure hope so." The broadcast tried to cover over the incident and continue. But Jackson had made his statement—and had made it through music.

Pop Goes the Country

Country music has its roots deep in American folk culture, but ever since Ralph Peer brought his tape recorder to Bristol, Tennessee, with the aim of turning this Appalachian music into something to *sell,* in mass quantities, country music has been in tension with the pop culture. The latter is a twentieth-century phenomenon made possible by the new media technologies, which allows works of art to be mass-produced and turned into a commodity to be bought and sold in the free market.

Originally, music was something people did, gathering around the parlor after dinner to sing and strum the old songs. Now it has become something people buy. Talented musicians profited, of course, but the studios, the record companies, the music industry, inevitably had their say. The engine that drives the pop culture is the marketplace, and the people who do the buying—the consumers—ultimately determine success and failure in the music business. Music that is too difficult, too demanding, or makes people feel too uncomfortable may not sell in the numbers studios need to make the highest profit.

On television—the supreme pop culture medium—whether a program gets renewed depends on one thing and one thing alone: ratings. The quality of a program, its artistic integrity, the valuable insights it conveys, make no difference to its success or failure. If the masses watch it, for whatever reason, it is termed a success. Conversely, though high quality work can, in fact, garner good ratings, the easiest route is to "give them what they want." Sex appeal, a few explosions, the latest fashions, all get people to tune in. Demanding too much reflection will lose the channel-surfing audience; raising controversial issues—such as religion—will turn people off.

Nearly all artists, including rock and roll stars and TV producers, now complain about how commercialism interferes with their work. Artists, by virtue of their talent, skill, and creativity, represent "high culture." When an artist's work is shaped not by a desire for artistic expression but by the demands of the public, the public, in effect, has taken over the work.

Whereas rock and roll moves easily with the changing fashions of popular tastes—so that rock and roll in general is often classified simply as pop music—it is a different story for country music. Country music, though in the commercial business of selling records, is also highly traditional, insofar as it is part of a continuing American folk culture.

Kenneth Myers, who discusses these different levels of culture in his book *All God's Children and Blue Suede Shoes,* says that both folk cultures and high cultures tend to be timeless, whereas pop culture focuses on the new. Folk and high cultures emphasize ability; pop culture emphasizes celebrity. The folk and the high are communal; pop is individualistic. Both folk and high art are allusive, encourage reflection, and offer a complex emotional, intellectual, and aesthetic experience; pop art is immediately accessible, lacks ambiguity, and calls forth an instant, nonreflective response.[1]

"Folk culture," says Myers, "while simpler in manner [than high culture] and less communicable from one folk to another, has the virtues of honesty, integrity, commitment to tradition, and perseverance in the face of opposition."[2] These values of folk culture—which are the values of country music—are in conflict with the values of pop culture. In place of honesty, commercial art values artifice, appearance, and rhetorical manipulation. In place of integrity, pop culture is infinitely flexible, unprincipled, and open to anything. In place of commitment to tradition, pop culture has a commitment to fashion, in which products must go in and out of style very quickly so that people will keep buying. In place of perseverance in the face of opposition—Myers gives as an example the African-American spirituals—the pop culture always goes with the flow.

One could argue that all three levels of culture have their own validity, but the problem, Myers goes on to show, is that in the late twentieth century, pop culture has been pushing out and taking the place of the other two. Just as high culture institutions such as schools and universities are having problems teaching young people who can pay attention only if they are • **163** being entertained, folk cultures around the world are disappearing under the onslaught of American TV, movies, consumer goods, and fast-food restaurants. In religion, many people today have no interest in the high culture of theological reflection, nor in the folk culture of ancient practices and old hymns; rather, they are cultivating a pop Christianity void of doctrine and unpleasant moral demands, centered instead on individualistic emotional gratification. Instead of achieving conversions through conviction of sin and proclaiming the blood of the Lamb, evangelism is sometimes reduced to what is, in effect, a commercial appeal.

Country music has always had an ambivalent relationship to pop music. All performers want a hit record, and crossing over from the community of country music fans to reach the even larger audience enjoyed by pop music has always been a coup. Patsy Cline crossed over to the pop charts. Her appeal was and is universal. Almost everyone, no matter what kind of music one prefers, is bowled over by the vocal performances of Patsy Cline. And country music as a whole has certainly influenced pop music, as in the rockabilly roots of Elvis Presley.

But as television, entertainment conglomerates, and new audiences began to impact the music industry in the last decades of the twentieth century, tunes on the country charts began to sound indistinguishable from those on the pop charts. Again, with the song "I Can Love You Like That," John Michael Montgomery did it with a slight twang, while All-4-One, an African-American group, did it with rhythm and blues stylings. But there was not much difference in the way it sounded. This was not really a matter of crossing over (except perhaps for the songwriters). The musicians played to separate audiences and appealed to separate markets.

One factor in the conjunction of country and pop was doubtless the rise of music videos. With the advent of MTV, music was no longer just something heard on the radio—it was something to watch. The visual images accompanying the sound were, in effect, a new art form. It was certainly a new marketing form, as a hot video generally led, ironically, to more radio play and certainly to bigger sales. MTV, though, was for rock audiences.

But by the 1980s, country had a parallel video presence on cable TV, TNN (The Nashville Network), and when that cable channel began leaning more heavily on TV stereotypes of Southern culture, such as *The Dukes of Hazzard* and *Dallas* reruns, the all-music CMT (Country Music Television) came into being.

To be sure, there are major differences between rock videos and country videos. MTV's rock videos tend to be fragmented and surreal, with fast cuts, visual rhythms, and imagery that is striking but does not make a lot of sense. Country videos naturally tend to be narratives, reflecting the storytelling character of the music. They range from more or less faithful renditions of the song lyrics to narrative sequences that don't quite go with the song, but still in some way tell a story. The editing is much more unified and visually coherent. The imagery is often from small towns or farms and features ordinary people (as in Shania Twain's video, where she vamps for wide-eyed men in an actual diner, asking them "Whose Bed Have Your Boots Been Under?" as if they were her boyfriends).

Country videos, however, also contributed to the peculiar cult of celebrity that defines the television age. Being photogenic became an important attribute of the would-be country star. The look became as important as the sound—or potentially even more so, since electronic wizardry in the recording studio can always adjust the way a performer sounds. Male hat acts had to be handsome, in a generic sort of way. A premium was placed on gorgeous women. Sometimes fans became so infatuated with particular celebrities that the music came second.

But the major reason country became more and more influenced by pop was the huge new audience that had recently discovered country music, an audience that was not mainly rural or working class, an audience that had grown up on rock and roll. And the reason for this vast, new, though pop-leaning audience was one man.

Garth Brooks: Bigger than Elvis

Garth Brooks is a singer from Yukon, Oklahoma, who got his start in the college town of Stillwater. But from the time of his **· 165** first album, *No Fences,* in 1989, he managed to break through to the vast, mass audience of Americans of all stripes, introducing them to country music and giving country music its biggest market share ever. During the following decade, he had sold 95 million albums, surpassing even Elvis Presley in record sales, ranking second only to the Beatles—and still climbing.

In many ways, Garth was an unlikely superstar. Somewhat pudgy and balding, lacking a strong, distinctive voice, Garth nevertheless was full of stage charisma and exhibited an almost unerring ability to pick material. And though his detractors do not always give him credit for this, Garth's early, fence-breaking records were truly country.

He offered fresh, often witty, renditions of the great country music motifs. He did songs about social class, with the old motif of a working man rising above his background with a high-class woman—showing up in boots at a former girlfriend's black-tie wedding reception, consoling himself that "I've Got Friends in Low Places." He recorded guilt-ridden cheatin' songs ("Thunder Rolls"), as well as earthy celebrations of marriage ("We're Two of a Kind, Workin' on a Full House"). And he brought back into the American imagination songs about cowboys and rodeos ("Rodeo").

Brooks also sang unself-consciously about God, in that country way that ties faith to ordinary life. He did an allegory about life as a boat, called "I Will Sail My Vessel," in which he makes it clear that he is sailing "with the good Lord as my captain." Most notable was the previously discussed "Unanswered Prayers," which has an honest charm and raises real-life issues of God's providential design—how momentary disappointments may hide God's higher and better plan, how as human beings we may not know what is best for ourselves. He thanks the Lord "for the gifts in my life."

Garth's music touched a chord with people beyond the usual audience of country music. And these were country chords. The charm and authenticity and time-honored motifs rang true for *fin de siècle* Americans of nearly all demographics, across generational and cultural lines.

Garth's music was accessible to this audience in a way hard-core country artists might not be. His singing was relatively twang-free—his middle-class Oklahoma accent was enough to give his voice a certain down-home appeal, without the heavy Southern drawl that to many Americans, unfortunately, spelled "Hicksville." His songs were fresh, hipper takes on old country music themes. To this day, Garth Brooks remains a good introduction to country music for the not-yet-initiated.

But Garth didn't grow up with country. He has said that he used to be a fan of Kiss and other heavy metal rock bands, with their painted faces, outrageous stage personas, and concerts filled with lasers, special effects, and explosions. He turned to country, he said, when he discovered George Strait, the clean-cut cowboy with the great melodies who ignited the New Traditionalist movement in the 1980s. Garth idolized Strait—to the point of always leaving a pair of tickets at the window, to all of Brooks' sold-out shows, just in case George Strait shows up. But there is probably a reason why Strait has never appeared: Garth brought the Kiss aesthetic to his stage shows.

Brooks has sometimes made his appearance by rappelling onto the stage or by soaring across the arena over his screaming fans, like Tinkerbell on a wire. He brought smoke, explosions, big screens, and spectacle into the country music concert, using them to heighten his own energetic, charismatic performances. To the rock-arena atmosphere, however, he also brought the endearing custom that country performers have of honoring their audiences. Well after he became a megastar, Garth once signed autographs for a whole day, refusing to leave until he met every fan. The millionth fan to attend one of his concerts was regaled with a new truck, and every millionth fan after that receives more and more prizes. And Garth poured himself out to put on a good show. The fans responded with affection and loyalty. His free concert in New York City—hardly what one would think of as a country music mecca—brought hundreds of thousands of people to Central Park, setting a record for the Big Apple.

In 1992, Garth's idol, George Strait, starred in the movie *Pure Country*. Although the plot is thin—a country music star (Strait) temporarily abandoning his hectic life as a performer to find true love—the film was also a commentary on the changes in country music. The country star longs to play a Texas road-house instead of large auditoriums, and when the incognito star visits his grandmother, she tells him that she had attended a recent concert and couldn't make out the words. She has other criticisms, all pointed toward the rock-arena music scene that country music had adopted. At the film's conclusion, Strait's character wins the girl in a concert that has eliminated the light show, the smoke machines, and the overblown production. Strait's movie seems to offer the opinion that country was los-ing its way by becoming something it was not. And the "impure country" Strait was targeting was clearly the brave new world inaugurated by Garth Brooks.

But it was hard for Nashville to argue with success, espe-cially success on such a scale. The whole industry grew. More radio stations adopted the country format, more Garth-like stars were born, and more albums were sold. The Nashville record companies got bigger and bigger; they merged, acquired each other, or were acquired by even bigger corporations. The business aspect of it all frustrated many country artists—includ-ing Garth Brooks. At one point, he refused to release his next album, unless the head of Capitol Records–Nashville was removed and replaced by someone he liked. He was one of the few who had the clout to actually fulfill the artist's dream of standing up against the corporate masters.

But the vast new audiences, the influx of new money, and the commercial competitiveness of the music industry pulled country music in the direction of pop. The frenzy for fresh young celebrities meant there was little room or airplay for the older performers, who traditionally could perform and get air-play well into their golden years.

In the meantime, Garth himself began drawing more and more on the pop culture. He recorded a rather explicit song about a teenager's first sexual experience ("That Summer"). He did a song that seemed to call for gay rights, how people should be free to love whomever they want ("We Shall Be Free"). Con-servative fans squirmed at these incursions of what seemed like rock-culture promiscuity. He covered "The Fever," a song by the hard-rock group Aerosmith—at least it was a rodeo song. He made a hit of a new Bob Dylan tune, "To Make You Feel My Love"—which didn't seem too unbefitting, because Dylan veers toward country sometimes, and this was another example of Brooks' fine choice of material. But sometimes he sounded like Jimmy Buffett ("Give Me Two Piña Coladas").

And then the oddest thing happened. Garth created a fictional identity for himself and recorded a pop album.

But instead of creating an alter ego like Hank Williams' Luke the Drifter or Ferlin Huskey's rube character Simon Crum, Garth Brooks, in one huge leap, publicly embraced a completely different look and a different style of music: He became Chris Gaines, a rock star. It was a rare step of career miscalculation. The shrieks of glee and the merciless mocking emanating from Brooks' critics and detractors over such an odd and self-destructive change had not been so pointed for a musician since rock musician Prince demanded that his name be replaced by an unpronounceable symbol earlier in the decade. For Brooks to adopt the persona of a rock star made him seem less sincere and raised the question (that some purists had already been asking) of whether Garth really wanted to be a rock and roll singer. Garth's persona cast doubt on his country identity.

Postmodern Country Music

The end of the millenium was the postmodern age. In the last decades of the twentieth century, what was once hailed as modern became old-fashioned. Modern art, modern architecture, modern science, modern thought, and modern theology all became passé. On a deeper level, the assumptions that drove the twentieth century—that scientific rationalism is the only acceptable form of truth; that social engineering can solve all of our problems; that progress, reason, and realism will stamp out religious faith—came unglued. The promised utopias never came, sophisticated scholarship began taking apart the foundations of rationalism, and the legacies of the sixties set a whole generation in reaction to their parents' modernity.

Postmodernism took different forms and manifested itself in different ways. If what is modern is no longer seen as great, one response is to recover what is old and bring it into the contemporary times. Old buildings that survived modernism's urban renewal were restored to their formal splendor, and new houses began to be built following Victorian designs (with all of the high-tech conveniences inside, however). Historical novels came back, as did costume-drama movies (with *Titanic*—almost a parable of the shipwreck of modernism—surpassing *Star Wars* as the most successful movie ever). In the meantime, confessional, orthodox, historic Christianity came back in force, as the modernist theology of mainline liberals grew increasingly anemic and irrelevant. This cultural mood was doubtless one of the reasons country music—with what Bill Monroe called its "ancient tones"—came back into fashion as it did.

But there were other ways to be postmodern, which in many ways overwhelmed the neoconservativism. If scientific rationalism can never give us the certainty of truth, as many scholars in the universities were arguing, then maybe we can never apprehend truth. Maybe we can do without it. For many postmodernist scholars, truth is a construction—a provisional paradigm, manufactured by our culture or by ourselves. The premodernists believed in moral and intellectual absolutes, grounded in a transcendent God; modernists believed that truth is only what we can perceive empirically; the postmodernists believed that we make our own truths.[3]

This sort of academic speculation might seem esoteric, with little to offer ordinary people living—in Alan Jackson's terms—"here in the real world." But cultural, intellectual, moral, and religious relativism soon permeated every level of American culture. In 1991, 66 percent of Americans—two out of three—agreed that "there is no such thing as absolute truth."[4] Statements such as "That may be true for you, but it isn't true for me" became commonplace. Moral issues—from sex to abortion to euthanasia—began to be seen solely in terms of choice, a matter not of ethical principles but of choosing "what's right for *you*."

Postmodernist relativism was carried by the pop culture, not only in its impermanence but in its way of reducing everything—including serious matters such as politics—to a consumer choice. Even Christianity, despite the new confessionalism, found new expression as a pop religion, its doctrinal and moral truths and ancient traditions often toned down to fit the demands of the religious marketplace. New megachurches sprang up, featuring pop music instead of hymns, self-help tips instead of sermons, and entertainment instead of worship.

These cultural trends worked their way into country music as well. It is one thing for university professors to discuss the indeterminacy of meaning, but when postmodernist hermeneutics found their way into a country song, it was clear that relativism had made deep inroads into the worldview of ordinary Americans. As noted earlier, the group Diamond Rio recorded "It's All in Your Head," depicting a son reminiscing about his paranoid father, a snake-handling preacher. "We never walked on the moon, Elvis ain't dead/I ain't goin' crazy, it's all in my head." The refrain is a sophisticated postmodern critical theory: "It's all interpretation."

For postmodernists, truth is just a matter of personal interpretation; that is to say, we construct personal models in our minds to organize and account for the data that we perceive. Facts can be accounted for in any number of ways, and—as conspiracy theorists demonstrate—many different and elaborate explanatory paradigms can be constructed, each with its own self-contained plausibility structures. We saw men walk on the moon, but how do we know it wasn't staged in a TV studio? The papers said that Elvis died, but what if he were involved in a drug sting for the FBI, who then staged his death and moved him into the witness protection program? Notice that picture of Elvis with President Nixon, signing up as a special narcotics agent? And why does the gravestone at Graceland misspell his middle name?

Many people believe these very things, and any contrary evidence that is offered can be accounted for in terms of the conspiracy. Not that postmodernist scholars buy into these kinds of conspiracies—they reserve such arguments to make the case for cultural or religious relativism. But the bottom line is that "it's all interpretation." And "it's all in my head."

It isn't clear whether Diamond Rio's song embraces or parodies this kind of thinking. After all, at the end of the song, "Daddy took up a snake," whose bite, it turned out, was stronger than Daddy's faith. Contrary to the power-of-positive-thinking theology of pop Christianity—which views faith as the capacity to change reality by mind-power, rather than faith as trust in Christ—in this song objective reality broke in, and the snake killed him. Postmodernist solipsism has a way of running up against hard, cold, objective reality. Rattlesnake bite. Interpret that.

A song recorded by Patty Loveless, "The Trouble with the Truth" (Gary Nicholson) takes a more honest view, showing both the allure and the self-deception of relativism that denies objective truth. "Oh the trouble with the truth/Is it's always the same ol' thing." And yet, it's "impossible for me to change." As much as she complains about the truth, she comes to realize that she needs to face it. "And the trouble with the truth/Is it's just what I need to hear." It ruins "the taste of the sweetest lies." It comprises "every sin that I deny." The truth is everything she wants but also everything she fears.

The truth that is so troubling, of course, has nothing to do with the moon walk or with Elvis. It has to do, among other things, with sin, which hangs around despite any denial. In this song, the vogue of denying truth is unmasked as just an evasion. "I run and hide," she sings, "but there's always another test."

Country music tends to be in touch with contemporary culture. But due to country's traditionalism, it also remains ambivalent to this culture. Country songs sometimes embody or critique aspects of postmodernism in different ways. Postmodernist literary theory—which says that since all truth is a construction there is no real difference between fiction and nonfiction—has given rise to artistic styles such as "magical realism," in which extreme fantasy is worked seamlessly into a work of extreme realism. This style, used to great effect by Latin American writers such as Gabriel García Márquez, found its way into movies (as in *Groundhog Day*), commercials (a good number of beer ads), and nearly every video on MTV. This technique has also shown up in country songs, such as Mary-Chapin Carpenter's "I

Feel Lucky," which combines brand names and working girl angst with horoscopes, a voice from heaven, a winning lottery ticket, and cameos from Dwight Yoakam and Lyle Lovett.

Postmodernists also insist that our beliefs are merely matters of cultural convention and that literary plots, themes, and effects—including the techniques of realism—are also just matters of convention, devices repeated with variations in story after story down through the centuries. This has led many postmodernist writers to play with such conventions—murder mysteries, westerns, science fiction, horror movies—in exaggerated, self-conscious, and ironic ways. In country music, this manifests itself in acts such as BR–549—named from the phone number of Junior Sample's used-car dealership on *Hee Haw*—whose act includes exaggerated hillbilly personas complete with bib overalls. Their songs are faithful, if ironic, renditions of the time-honored conventions of country music—from the harmonies to the drinking, cheating, and sentimental subjects that have been repeated to the point of cliché. This approach, delightful in its own way, is one strain of what has come to be called alternative country.

Another corollary of postmodernism has to do with psychology. Modernist psychology focused on the "integration of the self" and the need to forge a strong identity and sense of self. Postmodernists, having rejected the objectivity and stability of truth, also reject the objectivity and stability of the self. In his book *The Protean Self,* the psychologist Robert Jay Lifton argues that the truly healthy person is one who can always change his identity. Like the mythical Proteus, who could change shapes so fast that Hercules could never quite get a handle on him, the postmodern man never lets himself be restricted by a single set of beliefs, relationships, or character traits. Rather, he is always reinventing himself.[5] Whereas modernist psychology worried about multiple-personality disorders, schizophrenia, and people needing to pull themselves together to forge a strong unified identity, in postmodernist psychology, identity-shifting is hailed as a sign of mental health.

Going through many different marriages, many different jobs, and many personality changes are all good things, accord- • **173** ing to postmodernist psychology. Those who are dysfunctional, according to Lifton, are those who are inflexible and dogmatic, committed to a particular belief system and letting it run their lives. Such people Lifton terms "fundamentalists"—a clear shot at Christians, whom he would classify as mentally ill.

Lifton was the first to hail President Clinton as "our first postmodern president," free of the constraints of ideology and belief in some objective truth, always reinventing himself according to the needs of the moment. Role-playing games have become a hallmark of postmodern culture, letting bookworms pretend to be medieval warriors—or vampires or witches or mass murderers. Internet surfers often assume a different identity for each screen name, with men pretending to be women, normally nice guys putting on a belligerent front, and solid family men acting like sex-crazed seducers. Or maybe it is sex-crazed seducers who are putting on the disguise in their regular lives as solid family men. The anonymity of the internet allows people to do what they would never do in the personalities known by their families and friends—use pornography, tell lies, flame the innocent with profanity and invective. But according to Lifton, the personalities known by families and friends are likewise constructions, so that we really are different people when we are with different groups. We have no self. We are free to be—to use another cliché—whoever we want to be.

In 1999, Garth Brooks decided to reinvent himself. He was not yet bigger than the Beatles. So he decided to become a rock star too. He did this by creating a new parallel identity for himself. Garth reinvented himself as someone he called Chris Gaines.

On the cover of his CD entitled *The Life of Chris Gaines,* Garth has given up his cowboy hat and western shirt. He has long hair pulled down nearly to his eyes and a little beard under his lip, and he stares out with a doomed look. The name came from a movie entitled *The Lamb,* a project Garth was involved in, about the death of a rock star. The album is supposedly Chris Gaines' greatest hits, a survey of his pop styles over the course of his career. But Garth was not content merely to record an album based on a movie he was in. He went on to construct a whole biography of this alter ego. Gaines was supposedly born in Australia to a pair of Olympic swimmers. With his band, Crush, he scored a series of hit records that range in style from the Beatlesque, through rhythm and blues, to the grungy depths of alternative rock. One of his albums was entitled *Fornucopia*. Gaines suffered a nearly fatal car wreck. Like other pop icons, he died young. (The movie was to be about whether Gaines had been murdered.)

This elaborate fiction and playacting allowed Garth to record pop songs—something country purists complained that he had been doing all along. But this was no mere nom de plume, such as Luke the Drifter or Simon Crum. The Chris Gaines identity was worked out in realistic detail and openly presented as an artifice. Garth's name appeared on the album along with the alias: "Garth Brooks as Chris Gaines." Hank Williams used Luke the Drifter as a way to sing the kind of songs that were closest to his heart. Ironically, the persona allowed him to set aside his celebrity and his image so that he could express his religious and moral beliefs more honestly. Garth and Chris, on the other hand, represent just two styles and two celebrities inhabiting the same body.

The effect was unsettling for country fans. Was the down-home everyman with friends in low places, whose impression of sincerity fans had always found endearing, also nothing more than a fictional role he was playing? After all, Garth had always had the curious habit of referring to himself in the third person—as in "Garth Brooks is going to put on a good concert"—as if he were someone different than himself.

As it turned out, *The Life of Chris Gaines* was the one album by Garth Brooks that bombed. The pop crowd didn't buy it, even though Chris Gaines nailed the sounds from rhythm and blues to alternative rock—no doubt because they knew it was by a country star. And country fans didn't buy it. They loved Garth Brooks not just for his own sweet self but for the music—for his country music. They wouldn't uncritically follow him for his celebrity alone. At least on some level, he had to keep it country, which—for all of the blurred boundaries—did need to be perceptibly different from the other genres of rock and pop. Country music fans, when it came down to it, prized authenticity and needed their music to seem real. By the end of the century, the boundaries of country music were starting to get clear again.

No Depression

At the same time country music was headed down the pop highway, something else happened simultaneously. To understand it, one must attend to what was happening in country's archrival and near relation—rock and roll. In the 1970s and 1980s, a number of young musicians—sick of the phoniness of commercial rock—started paring the music back to its most elemental form: loud, simple chords and driving rhythms. They cultivated an attitude too, an angry, cynical nihilism in their lyrics, that gained them the label "punks." The punk rockers were the children of the flower children and were reacting against all that sappy peace-and-love talk (as they considered it) with cold rage. Their fathers let their hair grow long and wore bright-colored tie-dye T-shirts; the punks cropped their hair to their skulls and wore black leather. Their parents were into what was natural; the punks dyed their hair bright colors and pierced their bodies. The hippies waved their arms like daisies when they danced; punk rockers danced by slamming into each other and knocking each other down.

On one level, the punk rockers were just another symptom of larger cultural confusions. They too, no less than the hippies or the metalheads or the glam rockers, were poseurs putting on a role, not nearly as nihilistic as they pretended to be. And yet, their particular reaction against the excesses of the pop culture had another dimension. They were sick not only of the phoniness of the pop culture, which in many cases was the only culture they had ever known; they were also sick of the phoniness of their postmodern times. Is it true that reality is just a construction of the culture and a front for economic manipulation shaped by power structures? If so, there is nothing to do but rebel against just about everything. But isn't there anything real? Anything that is not phony? In their quest for authenticity, the punk rockers plunged into the gritty and the sordid, into elemental emotions and transgressions.

But in the punk rockers' search for something real—as punk music itself became captive to the big recording studios that were making lots of money from punk angst, as punkdom was reduced to a fashion statement, and as they grew up a little—a number of former punk fans and performers pursued authenticity to the point that they broke through into country music.

In 1990, three young musicians from Belleville, Illinois—Jay Farrar, Jeff Tweedy, and Mike Heidorn—rechristened their rock band "Uncle Tupelo." (No one can say why, except that Elvis was from Tupelo, Mississippi.) They released an album called *No Depression*. The title came from an old Carter Family song, which they performed on the album. The song, credited to A. P. Carter, is not one of the Carter Family's old folk tunes; rather, it is a commentary on the Great Depression. Just as the Louvin Brothers used the atomic bomb as a way to contemplate the Apocalypse in "The Great Atomic Power" (a song Uncle Tupelo would also record), the Carters used the economic collapse of the 1930s to reflect on the judgment of God. These are the latter days, says the song, and "the hearts of men are failing." "The Great Depression now is spreading," which was evident at the time, but A. P. thinks it is a fulfillment of prophecy. "God's Word declared it would be so." Perhaps the economic catastrophe—in which people were losing their farms and leaving their homes to roam the country in search of work—was the beginning of the great tribulation. The song soon moves from the economic level to something deeper:

> This dark hour of midnight nearing
> And tribulation time will come.
> The storm will hurl in midnight fear
> And sweep lost millions to their doom.

But these harrowing images in the verses are countered by an upbeat chorus. As in other old country gospel songs, the travails of this world point ahead to the joys of the next:

> I'm goin' where there's no depression,
> To the lovely land that's free from care.

·177

I'll leave this world of toil and trouble.
My home's in heaven, I'm going there.

Uncle Tupelo was never perceived as a particularly religious band, though they occasionally sang songs similar to this one. The rest of the album is much closer to rock than to country, though their next three albums became ever closer to country as time went on.

Uncle Tupelo attracted a zealous following and many imitators. The style of music even became known as No Depression. The phrase, of course, had few associations with the stock market crash of 1929. Depression was used in its psychological meaning. To say "No Depression" was to say no to the reigning mood. Punk music was extremely depressing, as was its later offspring Grunge. So was much of contemporary life. A. P. Carter was showing the way to a kind of music that acknowledged the "dark hours" without sinking into the impotent ennui of giving up. It was a musical way out of nihilism, into a realm that was human, down-to-earth, and that seemed honest and real. Many of those pursuing authenticity discovered it in country music.

In the 1990s, as country music was becoming more commercial and more indistinguishable from pop music, another strain was emerging that was emphatically not commercial and that self-consciously resisted the pop culture influence. No Depression was by no means the only strain of what came to be known as alternative country. Austin, Texas, continued to be a center of experimental country music that soon went by this term. The retro fad and the roots rock movement—attempts to go back into the past to dredge up things of value for the present—played their part. Original pure-country artists who were too much for country radio got tagged with the alternative country label. Among such artists were Junior Brown, the closest thing country music has to Jimi Hendrix on the electric and the steel guitar; Wayne Hancock, with his Hank Williams–style voice and his 1940s sensibility; and Asleep at the Wheel, with their contemporary redactions of western swing.

Alternative country is too weak of a term for some. "Insurgent country" seems more appropriate, at least for the groups centered in Chicago, which might be considered a strange place for a center of any kind of country music. But Bloodshot Records started turning out music by the anarchic Waco Brothers and the lethally tongued satirist Robbie Fulks. This underground country scene was alive, diverse, and full of creative juices.

An overarching term for this new strain of country music is "Americana." It consists of music that is either too radical or too traditional for country radio. Americana is now a category in many record stores and has even become a radio format, to be found on stations—or at least, programs on stations—scattered across the country.

Some fans of Uncle Tupelo—and the two groups the band members eventually split into, Son Volt and Wilco—pursued their enthusiasms on an internet discussion list, which they later spun off into a bimonthly magazine called, aptly enough, *No Depression*. Among features on classic country performers such as Dolly Parton and Ricky Skaggs, interviews with new talent such as Buddy and Julie Miller (who speak of their Christian faith), and the plethora of ads from independent labels providing an alternative to the Nashville hit machine, is a "Top 40" chart. Though the editors are conscious of the irony in tracking the sales of "noncommercial" music, the magazine's chart gives a sense of the range of Americana music.

Listed on *No Depression*'s chart are country stalwarts who are too old for hat-act music videos, but who are making some of the best music of their careers, such as Doc Watson, Del McCoury, and Johnny Cash. Also included are some artists who have occasional hits on the country charts but are nevertheless edgy enough and traditional enough to be accepted as Americana: Lyle Lovett, Dwight Yoakam, Alison Krauss. Even some rock and roll stars are allowed in, because of their rootsy styles and sense of authenticity: Bob Dylan, Bruce Springsteen, Tom Petty. There are the critically acclaimed maverick songwriters, such as Steve Earle and Lucinda Williams. And then there are the alternative country musicians, who sometimes sound more •**179** alternative than country: The Waco Brothers, Wilco, Son Volt. All of the listed artists, though, to one degree or another, keep up the traditions—and the worldview—of country music as described in this book.

Not that Americana is above reproach. In trying to be real, alternative country can be rude and crude, and there is often good reason—its language and subject matter—why it cannot be played on the radio. Some No Depression musicians play the postmodern game of exaggerating the country music conventions and turning them into something ironic, which of course keeps the songs from being real at all (though they might be humorous or pleasant to listen to precisely because of these conventions).

But Americana has room for Christianity too, of a distinctly down-to-earth, unsentimental, and undiluted kind. Representative are Buddy and Julie Miller, in the grand tradition, and the group 16 Horsepower. *World Magazine*'s music critic, Arsenio Orteza, has compared the group's unsettling Southern gothic religiosity not just to the novelist of shocking grace, Flannery O'Connor, but to something even more extreme, a Flannery O'Connor *character*. On the surface, their music does not sound particularly like country, but then they toss in a startling lyric, such as, in a song about witnessing to a lost friend, "Your eyes are as empty as my Savior's tomb."

At Americana's other extreme is the music of Gillian Welch, who goes back into American music just about as far as possible—to the Carter Family sound. The songs she writes also emulate the Carter Family's hard-edged mountain piety. In her album *Revival,* she has the character of an orphan girl singing about eventually meeting her family in heaven, "at God's table." In the meantime, she asks her "Blessed Savior" to "be my mother, my father, my sister, my brother." In "Tear My Stillhouse Down," she has a dying moonshiner warning the listener to "tell all your children that Hell ain't no dream." In "By the Mark," she sings about Jesus dying on the cross to pay for her sins and how, when she crosses over after death, she will know her Savior "by the mark where the nails have been."

In the year 2000, a controversial song began to get airtime: "Murder on Music Row," written by bluegrass artist Larry Cordle. Someone on Music Row—the site of Nashville's recording industry—committed murder. And the victim was country music. Money and the lust for fame "slowly killed tradition," something that deserves rough country justice: "And for that, someone should hang." The song becomes a no-holds barred diatribe against pop country, from the decline of fiddles and steel guitars in favor of drums and rock 'n' roll guitars to complaints about how Merle and Hank could never get on today's radio, and how the "Possum" (George Jones) was sent home. The song was recorded as a duet by George Strait and Alan Jackson, two stars too big to ignore. Ironically, "Murder on Music Row" was named "Vocal Event of the Year" at the 2000 CMA awards by a perhaps chastened and guilt-ridden industry.

Country music may keep getting murdered, but then—even in the new millennium—it keeps getting born again.

In the best of all of this music and the traditions it keeps alive, the despair and the hope, the suffering and the ordinary pleasures, all ring true. It can sometimes be tacky and vulgar and sentimental, but somehow that is part of its charm too. The music has a way of applying, no matter how often the culture changes. And the faith seems as authentic as the sinning.

Notes

Chapter 1: The Music of American Adults

1. Much of this chapter appeared in an earlier form as the cover story one of us wrote for *World Magazine,* 8 March 1997. The facts and statistics given here were researched from various sources for that article. The numbers are valid for 1997. Country's market share declined in 1999, but this was balanced by huge crossover sales, as discussed in chapter 10.

2. Songwriting credits are given in parentheses after the song titles. When no names are given in parentheses, that means the performer is also the writer of the song. In attending to lyrics and studying what they say, the ideas expressed are obviously those of the songwriter rather than the performer.

3. Johnny Cash, liner notes to *Unchained,* American.

Chapter 2: Gospel Music Origins

1. This point was made in a conversation with Gene Veith by Ronnie Pugh of the Country Music Foundation. See also Don Cusic, *The Sound of Light: A History of Gospel Music* (Bowling Green, Ohio: Bowling Green University Popular Press, 1990), 181.

2. Bill Malone, liner notes to *Country Gospel,* record 1 of *The Greatest Country Music Recordings of All Time,* The Country Music Foundation Official Archive Collection.

3. Dorothy Horstman, *Sing Your Heart Out, Country Boy* (Nashville: Country Music Foundation Press, 1996), 32, 38.

4. Ibid., 32.

5. Cusic, *The Sound of Light,* 181.

6. Malone, liner notes to *Country Gospel.*

7. See Thomas L. Wilmeth, *Heaven's Own Harmony: The Music of the Louvin Brothers* (Lewiston, N.Y.: Edwin Mellen, 1999). Wilmeth's book was based in part on extensive interviews with Charlie Louvin. References throughout

this present volume to the career of the Louvin Brothers and quotations from Mr. Louvin are drawn from Wilmeth's book.

8. Cusic, *The Sound of Light*, 181.

9. George Pullen Jackson, *White Spirituals in the Southern Uplands* (New York: Dover, 1933), 7–8.

10. Buell E. Cobb Jr., *The Sacred Harp: A Tradition and Its Music* (Athens, Ga.: University of Georgia Press, 1978), 3.

11. Quoted from Horstman, *Sing Your Heart Out*, 33.

12. Steve Spurgin, Songwriting Workshop, Oklahoma International Bluegrass Festival, Guthrie, Oklahoma, 1 October 1999.

13. Cusic, *The Sound of Light*, 177.

14. Malone, liner notes to *Country Gospel*.

15. Ibid.

Chapter 3: The Bristol Sessions

1. From the cover of *The Bristol Sessions*, Country Music Foundation.

2. Nolan Porterfield, *Jimmie Rodgers: The Life and Times of America's Blue Yodeler* (Urbana, Ill.: University of Illinois Press, 1992), 17.

3. Norm Cohen in Bill Malone and Judah McCullo, eds., *Stars of Country Music: Uncle Dave Macon to Johnny Rodriguez* (Urbana, Ill.: University of Illinois Press, 1975), 16.

4. The Tennessee Mountaineers' hymn about faith in Christ's promises is well rehearsed, but, in its lack of instrumentation, is stylistically at odds with almost all of the other recordings from Bristol. Peer recorded this group last, and somewhat hastily. While most groups took at least two-and-a-half hours, Peer spent a mere thirty minutes with the Tennessee Mountaineers.

5. Liner notes to *The Bristol Sessions*.

6. The harp-guitar was manufactured around the turn of the century by the Gibson Guitar Company. In a conversation with Thomas Wilmeth, Chet Atkins was asked if he had ever played in a recording session that included a harp-guitar. He replied, "I never have," and continued, "I don't even know how somebody would have played it." The self-accompanying effect that this large guitar was capable of was later perfected by Maybelle Carter on just the regular guitar, with her ability to play the single note melody on the bass strings while sweeping the higher strings for her own rhythm accompaniment.

7. Ed Kahn, liner notes to *The Carter Family on Border Radio from Radio Station XTE*, Monterray, NL Mexico, 1939. Vol. 1, Arhoolie, 411, 1995.

8. Liner notes to *The Bristol Sessions*.

9. Ibid.

10. Quoted in Ibid.

11. Porterfield, *Jimmie Rodgers*, 26.

12. Malone, liner notes to *The Smithsonian Collection of Classic Country Music*, 23.

13. Ironically, the Webb Pierce connection goes further, with Pierce having his biggest hit ever with a remake of Rodgers' "In the Jailhouse Now." When we speak of hit records, this refers primarily to record sales. There were, of course, no *Billboard* charts when Rodgers was at his peak, but he was a very popular performer and sold many records for Victor, the label

that ran the Bristol Sessions and that continued to record Rodgers' music for the rest of his life.

Chapter 4: Nashville

1. The only exception was when Bob Wills played the Opry after the war. As his band was setting up, he was told that he couldn't use his drums or horns. Wills immediately started packing up, whereupon the Opry official quickly gave him an exemption. See Charles R. Townshend, *San Antonio Rose: The Life and Music of Bob Wills* (Urbana, Ill.: University of Illinois Press, 1986), 102.

2. Interview by Bill Anderson, *Opry Backstage*, The Nashville Network, 19 February 2000.

3. Personal conversation with Thomas Wilmeth.

Chapter 5: The Christian Tradition in Country Music: Between the Devil and Me

1. Dave Shiftlett, "Holy and High Octane," *The Wall Street Journal*, 24 September 1999, W21.

2. Ibid.

3. Ronnie Pugh, liner notes to *Country Gospel*, record 2 of *The Greatest Country Music Recordings of All Time*, The Country Music Foundation Official Archive Collection.

Chapter 6: The Christian Tradition in Country Music: Old Ruined Churches

1. Harold Bloom, *The American Religion: The Emergence of the Post-Christian Nation* (New York: Simon and Schuster, 1992).

Chapter 8: Country Music's Moral Tradition: Drinkin', Cheatin', and Family Values

1. See Thomas L. Wilmeth, *Heaven's Own Harmony: The Music of the Louvin Brothers* (Lewiston, N.Y.: Edwin Mellen, 1999), 49.

Chapter 9: The Country Artist: Hank Williams versus Luke the Drifter

1. Roger M. Williams, *Sing a Sad Song: The Life of Hank Williams* (Urbana, Ill.: University of Illinois Press, 1980), 11.

2. Ibid., 160.

3. Collin Escott, liner notes to *The Complete Hank Williams*, 10 CD Set, Mercury Records 314 5360772 (1998), 33.

4. Hank Davis, liner notes to *Hank Williams: Lost Highway: December 1948–March 1949*, 2 LP Set, Polydor Records 825 554–1, 1986.

Chapter 10: Contemporary Country Music

1. Kenneth A. Myers, *All God's Children and Blue Suede Shoes: Christians and Popular Culture* (Wheaton: Crossway, 1989), 120.

2. Ibid., 59.

3. This is explained and explored in more depth in *Postmodern Times: A Christian Guide to Contemporary Thought and Culture* by Gene Edward Veith (Wheaton: Crossway, 1994).

4. George Barna, *The Barna Report: What Americans Believe* (Ventura, Calif.: Regal, 1991), 83–84.

5. Robert Jay Lifton, *The Protean Self: Human Resilience in an Age of Fragmentation* (Chicago: University of Chicago Press, 1999).

Credits
and Acknowledgments

Special thanks to Ronnie Pugh, archivist at the Country Music Foundation, for his input and suggestions and for giving us accesss to the Foundation's collection in Nashville.

We also thank the following publishers for giving us permission to quote their songs:

Bocephus Music, Inc. for "A Country Boy Can Survive"

Hal Leonard Corporation for "Hickory Wind"

Hendershot Music and Sydney Erin Music for "What If Jesus Comes Back Like That?"

McLachlan Scruggs International for "Passin' Thru"

O-Tex Music for "Love without End, Amen"

Peer Music for "The Wonderful City" © 1950, "Will the Circle Be Unbroken?" © 1935, "No Depression" ©1937, "Mom and Dad's Waltz" ©1951, "Keep on the Sunny Side" ©1928, "It Wasn't God Who Made Honky Tonk Angels" ©1952, "Blue Yodel #1" ©1928 by Peer International Corporation. Copyright renewed. International rights secured. Used by permission. All rights reserved.

Rites of Passage Music for "She's in Love with the Boy"

Sony/ATV Music Publishing LLC for "Brand New Man" ©1991, "Neon Moon" ©1994, "Don't Laugh at Me" ©1998, "Love's the Only House" ©1999, "I Think About You" ©1996, "Little Rock" ©1993, "Make the World Go Away" ©1963, "It's a Cheating Situation" ©1978, "Mama Tried" ©1968, "The Fightin' Side of Me" ©1970, "Hungry Eyes" ©1969, "If We Make It through December" ©1973, "The Farmer's Daughter" ©1971,

Credits and Acknwledgments

Gene Edward Veith is professor of English at Concordia University-Wisconsin, cultural editor of *World Magazine*, and the author of a number of books, including *Postmodern Times: A Christian Guide to Contemporary Thought and Culture* and *State of the Arts: From Bezalel to Mapplethorpe*. He resides in Cedarburg, Wisconsin.

Thomas Wilmeth is also professor of English at Concordia and has also written widely about country music, including *The Music of the Louvin Brothers: Heaven's Own Harmony*. He lives in Grafton, Wisconsin.